FLAUBERT'S "GUEULOIR"

MICHAEL FRIED

FLAUBERT'S "GUEULOIR"

ON *MADAME BOVARY* AND *SALAMMBÔ*

YALE UNIVERSITY PRESS • NEW HAVEN AND LONDON

Printed in China

Library of Congress Cataloging-in-Publication Data

Fried, Michael.
Flaubert's gueuloir : on Madame Bovary and Salambo / Michael Fried.
p. cm.
Includes bibliographical references and index.
ISBN 978-0-300-18705-2 (cl : alk. paper)
1. Flaubert, Gustave, 1821–1880–Technique. 2. Flaubert, Gustave, 1821–1880. Madame Bovary.
3. Flaubert, Gustave, 1821–1880. Salammbô. I. Title.
PQ2250.F75 2012
843'.8–dc23

2012007287

A catalogue record for this book is available from
The British Library

Frontispiece
Illustration by J. Touchet of the elephant *Fureur de Baal*
from the title page of the 1936 edition of Flaubert's *Salammbô*.

TO

JACQUES NEEFS

AND THE MEMORY OF

DANIEL ARASSE

CONTENTS

PREFACE

For a long time I cherished the idea of some day writing an essay on Flaubert's prose in *Madame Bovary*. What finally made it realistic to do so was the experience of teaching a seminar on *Madame Bovary* jointly with my colleague Jacques Neefs, James M. Beall Professor of French in the Department of German and Romance Languages and Literatures at Johns Hopkins University. It was not only Neefs's unsurpassed knowledge of Flaubert's manuscripts, the famous brouillons, and the entire critical literature that proved so enabling; more important were the brilliance and subtlety of his observations on the novel in class after class, along with his conviction, fully shared by me, that we were indeed dealing with a literary masterpiece of the very highest order. As I explain in the introduction, I then went on to write an essay on the remarkable novel that followed *Madame Bovary*, the still not sufficiently appreciated *Salammbô*. The present book comprises the two essays, which together put forward a single framework within which – this is my claim – Flaubert's stylistic enterprise during the 1850s and early 1860s may be understood.

In addition to Neefs, others who have contributed to my project in different ways are Jennifer Ashton, Howard Bloch, Jean-Pierre Criqui, Jonathan Culler, Ruth Leys, Leonardo Lisi, Walter Benn Michaels, Yi-Ping Ong, Robert B. Pippin, and Ralph Ubl. To Criqui and Neefs in particular I owe a sense of confirmation from two masterful native speakers, readers, and writers of French that my intuitions as to what goes on in *Madame Bovary* and *Salammbô* at a micro-textual level are not necessarily invalidated by my own limitations in those regards. Unless otherwise credited, all translations from the French are by Nils F. Schott, though of course the responsibility for their correctness is mine. (I have also had input here and there.) Once again my editor, Gillian Malpass, has done inspired work in making this book the intellectual object I would have it be. My sincere thanks to all. And of course I am grateful to Yale University Press for its willingness to publish an English-language book in which so much of the critical action takes place in French.

Flaubert's "Gueuloir" is dedicated to Jacques Neefs and to the memory of a superb art historian and warm-hearted friend, Daniel Arasse.

"Le Gueuloir": From *gueuler*, to yell. Flaubert's term for his regular practice of reading his sentences in a loud voice, as a means of becoming aware of defects in the writing (assonances, consonances, repetitions of all kinds) that he would then seek to eliminate in pursuit of a new and extremely demanding ideal of stylistic perfection.

INTRODUCTION

This book comprises two long essays, the first on Gustave Flaubert's *Madame Bovary* and the second on the novel he wrote immediately afterward, *Salammbô*.

To begin at the beginning: I first read *Madame Bovary* in French in my twenties, and from the opening pages I was struck, to the point of amazement, by the radical difference between Flaubert's prose in the original and in translation. That such a difference exists is hardly news, and *Madame Bovary* is by no means the only novel, much less the only work of literature, of which something of the sort is true. But I was on to a truth nevertheless, and over the years, in the course of multiple rereadings, I came to feel strongly – to risk a certain hyperbole – that *Madame Bovary* only exists as itself in French, and that all the English translations of it with which I am familiar, including the recent, excellent one by Lydia Davis, not only amount to more or less accomplished paraphrases of an incomparable original but also, more to my point in this book, necessarily fail to convey the least hint of the fine texture of the writing, I mean on the level not of paragraphs or sentences or memorable phrases but rather of individual words, even of individual phonemes, even, indeed, of individual letters, in which, to my mind, much of the uniqueness of *Madame Bovary* as a literary text ultimately resides. Put slightly differently, I came to regard *Madame Bovary* as a consummate literary artifact, one written all the way down, so to speak – but of course only in the language in which it was composed. In English translation (I do not presume to speak of translations into other languages, though I would be hard to persuade that the situation could be different there) all that remains is the somewhat banal story, the characterizations, artful but not absolutely compelling, of the various dramatis personae, and certain characteristic but necessarily general features of the author's manner of writing: for example, his predilection for free indirect style survives translation more or less intact, whereas his frequent use of the imperfect tense – so innovative in the original – often disappears from view.

In one sense, of course, all I am saying is that the true glory of *Madame Bovary* lies in its literary style, a point made by virtually every commentator going back to Flaubert himself in the many letters he wrote to his mistress Louise Colet between 1851 and 1856, the years during which he labored to compose his first masterpiece. And indeed the first essay in this book seeks to make a contribution to our understanding of Flaubert's conscious and sustained pursuit of a hitherto unachieved and indeed unaspired to "poetic" prose – a prose, moreover, that in its very perfection and musicality would establish itself as something other than the expression of the author's personal tastes and ideas (ideally it would be liberated from the author's "personality"). Equally important, however, that essay is also a study of aspects of Flaubert's prose that may be taken as escaping or resisting or even defying his drive for perfection, as he described that drive to Colet, the Goncourt brothers, and others. Take for example his determination to eliminate assonances, consonances, and repetitions of all sorts, in part by reading sentence after sentence at the top of his voice, until his lungs ached. According to Flaubert, that practice, called by him "le gueuloir," enabled him to detect such blemishes, which were then removed or changed in the interests of stylistic perfection. And yet it will be my claim that an extraordinary number of repetitions of all sorts in fact survive in passage after passage, and the question I go on to ask – it is, in effect, the question that drives everything that follows – is: What are we to make of this? What does it mean for our understanding of Flaubert's writerly achievement in *Madame Bovary* that his prose is intermittently, albeit not infrequently, shot through with precisely the sorts of phonemic effects that he claimed he wished to eliminate?

The first essay comprises nine parts plus a coda. In part one I begin by considering Flaubert's practice of the "gueuloir" as a crucial ingredient in his pursuit of stylistic perfection. I then go on to show how, as early as *Madame Bovary*'s first chapter, there are passages in which alliteration and other sorts of repetition play a conspicuous and, I suggest, highly surprising role. A brief account of the famous incident in the schoolroom in which the young Charles Bovary mumbles his name so that it comes out "Charbovari" leads to a discussion of the novelist and critic Jean Ricardou's contribution to a 1974 colloquium on "The Production of Meaning in Flaubert," in which Ricardou claims to detect various phonemic effects in Flaubert's treatment of the incident that, he further suggests, are in tension with the narrative (the words as such, the play of the signifier, put the novel as such into question). Following Ricardou's paper serious discussion followed, all of it recorded in the volume based on the conference; this is not the place to summarize the various points that were made, but I will say that it was in the course of that discussion that Roger Bismut followed up Ricardou's proposal that the name "Bovary" suggests the word "veau" by noting that that association belongs to a much larger concatenation of names and words, an entire "veau"-network one might say, that runs through the novel from first to last. (Jonathan Culler, developing that notion, has characterized this as the novel's "vealism.") Another connection that first emerged in Ricardou's paper was the association between the garbled name *"Charbovari"* and the word "charivari," a synonym for "vacarme" – the word used to characterize the students' response to Charles Bovary's performance – an association that has since become canonical in the secondary literature. Finally, the discussion also saw the emergence of the question as to how one is to understand the phonemic relations Ricardou claimed to have brought to light. In Françoise Gaillard's terms, what theory of the subject was implied by those relations, to the extent that they could be shown to exist? In response, Ricardou first sought to deflect the question and subsequently, in *Nouveaux problèmes du roman*, offered a quasi-psychoanalytic theory of how such relations might have come about, but in an important sense Gaillard's question remained unanswered. The first essay will take it up again.

In part two of that essay I go on to consider several other cruxes in important critical studies of Flaubert's text. The first of these, a recent monograph by a young German scholar Edi Zollinger, tries to show (successfully, to my mind) that throughout *Madame Bovary* there is at work a consistent pattern of allusions to Victor Hugo's 1831 masterwork, *Notre-Dame de Paris*. (One relatively trivial instance of this: Emma's dog, which goes missing in the course of the journey from Tostes to Yonville, is called Djali, the name, of course, of Esmeralda's goat.) The two other studies, deservedly admired essays by Jean Starobinski and Claude Duchet, call attention to passages in the novel that are marked by alliteration, assonance, and repetition, but, as I go on to say, "[both critics] are content for the most part to leave it not quite clear whether they consider those effects to have been consciously intended by the author or not."

At this point, and continuing in part three, I introduce what is likely to seem to the reader an excessively large number of specimen quotations from the novel – two in part two and no less than seventeen in part three – in order to demonstrate both the intrinsic character and the sheer frequency of the sorts of phonemic effects that I am claiming mark Flaubert's prose throughout *Madame Bovary*. Indeed the reader's patience is likely to be stretched thin: what is the point, he or she is bound to wonder, of all these citations, some of them not especially brief, presented one after another, culminating in an exchange drawn from the conversation between Charles and Rodolphe following Emma's death? Where are they tending and must there be so many of them? (Still more turn up further on in my text. My approach to literary criticism is no doubt influenced by my background in art history: as regards certain artists – Gustave Courbet and Adolph Menzel, for example – I favor many illustrations, precisely in order to show that the features of their work that seem to me most significant are in fact representative, not freak occurrences that prove nothing.) In part four, I try to respond to this reaction by briefly commenting on the passages in question, though the reader is likely to feel his or her patience further tried by my asking yet again how we are to understand the phenomena that by now are plainly in view. In particular I go on to raise the question as to what we are to make of them in light of the special role – quoting myself again – "that the notion of authorial intention or, say, will, 'volonté,' has always been understood to play in Flaubert's literary enterprise." Thus the clear import of Bismut's

observations following Ricardou's paper and of Culler's essays on
Flaubert's "vealism" (not, however, of Ricardou's remarks on the topic)
is that the entire "veau"-network was consciously and deliberately put in
place by the author. Similarly, the multiple allusions to various features
and incidents in *Notre-Dame de Paris* that Zollinger's monograph brings to
light can only have been intended as such by Flaubert. But what of the
altogether surprising frequency of the letter *v* – for "veau"? for Victor
Hugo? or both? – in many of the passages quoted in part three? It seems
inconceivable that most if not all of these could have been intended to
carry one or the other meaning; but is it absolutely certain that they are
all totally devoid of such an implication? How to account for them
remains a question.

Let this suffice by way of introduction to the first of the two essays.
I will simply say in addition that my argument proceeds by juxtaposing
to the structure of intention versus automatism or will versus nature that
I claim is at work in *Madame Bovary* an important but, until recently,
largely neglected philosophical text, Félix Ravaisson's *De l'habitude* (1838),
on the grounds that Ravaisson's view of the continuity between will and
nature, a continuity mediated and in a sense made intuitable by a particular conception of habit, precisely fits the phenomena I have been tracking in Flaubert's novel. (The title of the first essay could perhaps equally
well be "Will and Nature in *Madame Bovary*.") And I go on to comment
on the pertinence of Ravaisson's conception of habit to the painting of
Flaubert's contemporary, Gustave Courbet, an association first put
forward more than twenty years ago in my book *Courbet's Realism*. But
now my suggestion is that a common relation to a Ravaissonian conception of habit as mediating will and nature provides a hitherto unimagined
link between the respective achievements of the foremost French novelist and painter of their generation. The coda to the essay places a famous
set piece in *Madame Bovary* alongside one of Courbet's greatest paintings
and raises the possibility that the similarities between the two may
be more than coincidental. Finally, at several junctures in my text I make
use of two stunning critical essays on Flaubert by Marcel Proust and
Charles Du Bos, as well as, toward the end, of Proust's inspired pastiche

of Flaubert – but exactly how and to what purpose this is done will have to await the event.

The second essay, "Willing *Salammbô*," takes its departure from the first and tries to show not only that a different stylistic regime is in force – one in which will or intention, "volonté," seeks to expunge all traces of automatism and habit from the novelistic text – but also that this shift of ambition corresponds to a comparable revaluation of "volonté" and "le voulu" in the painting and art criticism of the early 1860s (with Edouard Manet the key figure), not that my references to those have anything of the scope of the discussion of Courbet late in essay one. (Charles Baudelaire's prose poems in *Le Spleen de Paris* turn out to be another relevant comparison.) Both essays, in other words, associate Flaubert's first two major novels with the painting of their time, but their emphasis remains squarely on his literary enterprise, with the aim of developing largely new terms in which the latter may be understood. I will only add, first, that although it was not part of my initial project to address *Salammbô*, I cannot now imagine the present book without the essay that seeks to come to grips with that extraordinary text and the retrospective light that is thereby thrown on my account of *Madame Bovary*; and second, that if that essay contributes in some small way to a wider recognition of *Salammbô* – for all its singularity – as an exemplary work of modern literature, I will regard *Flaubert's "Gueuloir"* as an unqualified success.

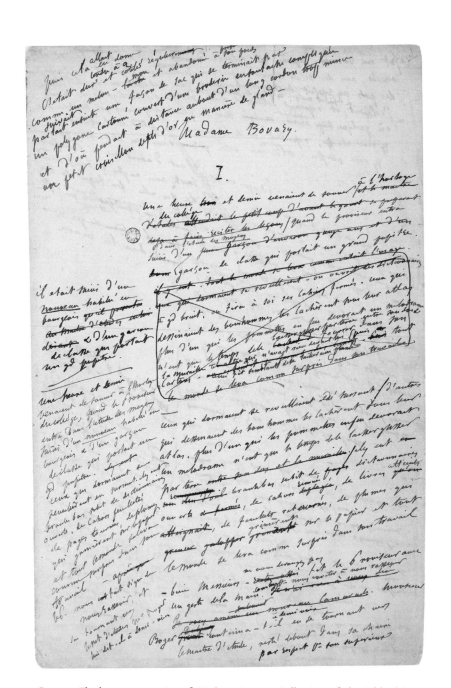

Gustave Flaubert, manuscript of *Madame Bovary*. Collection of the Bibliothèque Municipale de Rouen, MS g. 223 1 folio 3. Photo: Thierry Ascencio-Parry.

STYLE AND HABIT IN *MADAME BOVARY*

I envision a style: a style that would be beautiful, that someone will invent some day, ten years or ten centuries from now, one that would be rhythmic as verse, precise as the language of the sciences, undulant, deep-voiced as a cello, tipped with a flame: a style that would pierce your idea like a dagger, and on which your thought would sail easily ahead over a smooth surface, like a skiff before a good tail wind. Prose was born yesterday: you have to keep that in mind. Verse is the form par excellence of ancient literatures. All possible prosodic variations have been discovered; but that is far from being the case with prose.

> —Gustave Flaubert to Louise Colet[1]

Madame Bovary is first and foremost a book, a carefully composed book, amply premeditated and totally coherent, in which nothing is left to chance and in which the author or, better, the artist does exactly what he intends to do from beginning to end.

> —Charles-Augustin Sainte-Beuve[2]

Fundamentally and in fact, *Madame Bovary* – a masterpiece in its genre, the last word of truth in the novel – represents a very material side of art and thought. The accessories in it live as vividly and almost on the same level as the people. The physical setting is in such high relief around the feelings and passions that it almost stifles them. It is a work which paints for the eyes much more than it speaks to the soul. The noblest and strongest part of the book is much closer to painting than to literature. It is the stereopticon pushed to its furthest illusion.

> —Edmond and Jules de Goncourt[3]

Madame Bovary is not only *the* classical novel; it is also the only novel that can be called a work of art in the strict, precise, and one might say, narrow sense of the term.

–Charles Du Bos[4]

Flaubert . . . working with an irony impregnated with uncertainty, achieves a salutary discomfort of writing: he does not stop the play of codes (or stops them only partially), so that (and this is indisputably the proof of writing) *one never knows if he is responsible for what he writes* (if there is a subject *behind* his language); for the very being of writing (the meaning of the labor that constitutes it) is to keep the question *Who is speaking?* from ever being answered.

–Roland Barthes[5]

1

The critical literature surrounding Gustave Flaubert generally and *Madame Bovary* in particular is exceptionally rich and ingenious, but throughout there is universal agreement about his search for a new kind and degree of stylistic perfection in his first masterpiece. As is testified to by his correspondence during the years of composition (1851–6), this required prodigious and sustained effort, much of it spent at "le gueuloir," his term for his practice of reading manuscript pages in a loud voice to test them against an inner ideal. The classic account of the practice comes from his literary disciple Guy de Maupassant, who writes in an essay published after Flaubert's death:

> Sometimes, tossing the pen which he held in his hand into a large Oriental tin plate filled with carefully sharpened goose quills, he would take up a sheet of paper, raise it to the level of his gaze, and leaning on an elbow, declaim [its contents] in a loud, biting voice. He would listen to the rhythm of his prose, stop as if seizing a passing cadence, combine the tones, eliminate assonances, place the commas with exact knowledge, like the halting places on a long road.[6]

Maupassant goes on to quote two paragraphs from Flaubert's preface to his late friend Louis Bouilhet's *Dernières chansons*:

> A sentence is viable when it corresponds to all the necessities of breathing. I know that one is good when it can be read in a loud voice.
>
> Badly written sentences do not survive that test: they constrict the chest, impede the beating of the heart, and thus place themselves outside the conditions of life.[7]

It is sometimes said that the "gueuloir" was located in the garden of his property at Croisset,[8] but Maupassant's first-person account clearly locates the practice in Flaubert's study, which is not to say that he did not also take it outdoors. Of course, Maupassant, almost thirty years younger than Flaubert, came to know the latter only in the 1870s.

There are also brief but revealing allusions to the "gueuloir" in Flaubert's letters to his mistress, the poet Louise Colet, with whom he was in constant epistolary contact during most of the years of the composition of *Madame Bovary*. (Colet lived in Paris and was the recipient during the *Bovary* period of no fewer than 180 letters, in many of which Flaubert reports on his progress with his book and develops his literary aesthetic in considerable detail.) So for example on 21 March 1853 he wrote, "It is two in the morning. I thought it was midnight. I'm exhausted from having *guculed* [*gueulé*] all night as I was writing" (275; emphasis in original). And on 26 April: "It is quite late. – I'm very tired. My throat is raw from having shouted [*crié*] all night as I was writing, as is my extravagant habit" (315). From 1858, when he was at work on *Madame Bovary*'s successor, *Salammbô*, there are similar remarks in letters to Ernest Feydeau (28 August and 3 December 1858). Still another slightly later source is an entry in the Goncourts' *Journal* for 7 April 1861, in which they refer to "his mania for acting out and furiously declaiming the novel as he writes, shouting so much that he empties whole pitchers of water, intoxicating himself with his noise until he causes the metal plates, like the one here, to vibrate to such an extent that, one day at Croisset, he felt something hot rising from his stomach and was afraid that he was going to spit blood" (58).[9]

Flaubert's aim in such a practice, it seems clear, was to achieve a new sort of rhythmic musicality. As he wrote to Colet: "A good prose sentence should be like a good line of poetry – *unchangeable*, just as rhythmic, just as sonorous" (22 July 1852, Steegmuller, *Letters of Gustave Flaubert*, 1:166; emphasis in original)[10] – the effort to achieve which involved, as a practice of revision, seeking to eliminate disturbing assonances and repetitions. And a few days later, also to Colet: "It has now been seven or eight days that I've been at these corrections, and my nerves are very strained from it. . . . Finding in every sentence words to change, consonances to take out, etc., etc.! is arid, tedious, and at bottom very humiliating work" (26 July 1852).[11] Or again: "We only live by the outside of things. We must therefore take care of it. I for my part declare that the physical wins out over the moral. – No disillusion makes us suffer like a rotten tooth does, nor does an awkward statement get on my nerves like a creaking door. And that is why the best-intentioned of sentences spoils its effect as soon as it contains an assonance or a grammatical twist."[12] In the words of one of today's most devoted students and admirers of Flaubert, "this is French prose whose every syllable has been tested aloud again and again."[13]

Now consider a short passage from the first chapter of *Madame Bovary*. The new boy (or "*nouveau*"), Charles Bovary, has just caused an outbreak of hilarity in the classroom by the way in which, in response to the teacher's query, he has mangled his own name ("*Charbovari*"). Then we read:

> Cependant, sous la pluie des pensums, l'ordre peu à peu se rétablit dans la classe, et le professeur, parvenu à saisir le nom de Charles Bovary, se l'étant fait dicter, épeler et relire, commanda tout de suite au pauvre diable d'aller s'asseoir sur le banc de paresse, au pied de la chaire. Il se mit en mouvement, mais, avant de partir, hésita.
>
> –Que cherchez-vous? demanda le professeur.
>
> –Ma cas . . . [casquette], fit timidement le *nouveau*, promenant autour de lui des regards inquiets.[14]

But a shower of penalties gradually restored order; and the teacher, finally grasping the name Charles Bovary after it had been several times spelled out and repeated and he had read it aloud himself, at once commanded the poor devil to sit in the dunce's seat, at the foot of the platform. He began to move toward it, then hesitated.

"What are you looking for?" the teacher demanded.

"My c–" the new boy said timidly, casting an uneasy glance around him.[15]

My question, the first of many similar ones I shall be asking, is, what is the reader to make of so many words beginning with, and in one instance, "épeler," including, the letter *p*? Technically speaking, this does not amount to a case of assonances, which by definition chiefly concern the repetition of the same or similar vowel sounds. But in the penultimate citation from Flaubert's letters he specifically uses the term "consonances," which perfectly fits our excerpt, and in any case we are certainly dealing here with the phenomenon of repetition, supposedly another target of his obsessive revisions. As for the letter *p* itself, it is not one, it would seem, that could easily escape the notice of the "gueuloir." But is this right? Can we be absolutely certain that Flaubert would have been aware of so much seemingly excessive alliteration in a relatively small span of prose? I want to leave the question open, though I also want to add that if we are inclined to assume that at least on this occasion he must have been aware of what was taking place from word to word, we find ourselves under the intellectual obligation to try to motivate so seemingly bizarre a lexical choice on the part of a writer whose stylistic priorities, especially in *Madame Bovary*, have always been understood, partly on his own testimony, as tending in a quite different direction. (One possibility: he was aiming for a comic effect arising directly from so many *p*-words in close succession. But is this consistent with the perfectionism he elsewhere professes to be his ideal? Perhaps it is – but it would be a different sort of perfectionism than that usually attributed to him.)

This is not, of course, the only strangeness to be found in chapter one. To begin with, there is the opening sentence, with its highly problematic first word: "Nous étions à l'étude, quand le Proviseur entra, suivi d'un *nouveau* habillé en bourgeois et d'un garçon de classe qui portait un grand pupitre" (55) ["We were in the study-hall when the headmaster entered, followed by a new boy not yet in school uniform and by the handyman carrying a large desk" (3)] – the strangeness being the irruption of a "nous" at the very outset of a text that will soon banish that "nous" in favor of a rigorously impersonal mode of narration. (Also the way in which *"nouveau"* all but contains the word "nous." Significantly, that opening "Nous" was inserted by Flaubert at the latest possible moment – it appears in no brouillon, not even the so-called "definitive" one,[16] but is entered in the margin of the copyist's version of the final text.) Some pages later, a paragraph begins, "Il serait maintenant impossible à aucun de nous de se rien rappeler de lui" (63) ["It would be very difficult today for any of us to say what he was like" (10)], a statement immediately followed by a detailed account of Charles Bovary's years in the school, his medical training, his initial failure and then his passing the examinations for medical officer, his taking up a position in Tostes, and finally his marriage to an unappealing older widow.

Also in chapter one, just a half-dozen paragraphs into the narrative, we are given the famous description of Charles's "casquette":

> C'était une de ces coiffures d'ordre composite, où l'on retrouve les éléments du bonnet à poil, du chapska, du chapeau rond, de la casquette de loutre et du bonnet de coton, une de ces pauvres choses, enfin, dont la laideur muette a des profondeurs d'expression comme le visage d'un imbécile. Ovoïde et renflée de baleines, elle commençait par trois boudins circulaires; puis s'alternaient, séparés par une bande rouge, des losanges de velours et de poils de lapin; venait ensuite une façon de sac qui se terminait par un polygone cartonné, couvert d'une broderie en soutache compliqué, et d'où pendait, au bout d'un long cordon trop mince, un petit croisillon de fils d'or, en manière de gland. Elle était neuve; la visière brillait. (56–7)

> It was a headgear of composite order, containing elements of an ordinary hat, a hussar's bushy, a lancer's cap, a sealskin cap and a nightcap: one of those wretched things whose mute hideousness suggests unplumbed depths, like an idiot's face. Ovoid and stiffened with whale-

bone, it began with three convex strips; then followed alternating lozenges of velvet and rabbit's fur, separated by a red band; then came a kind of bag, terminating in a cardboard-lined polygon intricately decorated with braid. From this hung a long, excessively thin cord ending in a kind of tassel of gold netting. The cap was new; its peak was shiny. (4)

As innumerable commentators have remarked, the "casquette" is not an item of clothing that can be visualized by the reader, at least not as a whole.[17] Rather, it is a kind of hyperbolic or impossible object, a verbal tour de force more than a possible entity in the world; as such it anticipates the only somewhat less famous cake at the wedding dinner for Emma and Charles, and (further on and more briefly) the "ivoireries indescriptibles" ["indescribable ivories"] (447) made by Binet on his lathe. In any case, a reader who begins reading the previous passage in anticipation of a description of Charles's "casquette" such as might be encountered in a novel by Balzac would be seriously disconcerted.

Then there is the brief, vivid account of the scene that arose when Charles mumbled his name. At first, then once again, what he said was completely unintelligible.

> –Plus haut! cria le maître, plus haut!
>
> Le *nouveau*, prenant alors une résolution extrême, ouvrit une bouche démesurée et lança à pleins poumons, comme pour appeler quelqu'un, ce mot: *Charbovari*.
>
> Ce fut un vacarme, qui s'élança d'un bond, monta en *crescendo*, avec des éclats de voix aigus (on hurlait, on aboyait, on trépignait, on répétait: *Charbovari! Charbovari!*), puis qui roula en notes isolées, se calmant à grand-peine, et parfois qui reprenait tout à coup sur la ligne d'un banc où saillissait encore çà et là, comme un pétard mal éteint, quelque rire étouffé. (57–8) [There follows the paragraph beginning, "Cependant, sous la pluie des pensums . . ."]

"Louder!" cried the teacher. "Louder!"

With desperate resolve the new boy opened a mouth that seemed enormous, and as though calling someone he cried at the top of his lungs the word "Charbovari!"

This touched off a roar that rose *crescendo*, punctuated with shrill screams. There was a shrieking, a banging of desks as everyone yelled, "Charbovari! Charbovari!" Then the din broke up into isolated cries that slowly diminished, occasionally starting up again along a line of desks where a stifled laugh would burst out here and there like a half-spent firecracker. (50)

This too has become a famous crux in Flaubert studies thanks, in the first instance, to the novelist and critic Jean Ricardou, who in a 1974 paper delivered at a week-long conference in Cerisy on "The Production of Meaning in Flaubert" focused on what he took to be a kind of war between the words of the text and the novel proper, one in which it is the words themselves "that choose, even arrange, descriptions and narratives."[18] (Another term for this was "anagrammatization.") Here I have no choice but to quote Ricardou at length:

Let us sum up: a group of words, subjected to various manipulations of its sounds and letters, can induce new language occurrences to come about. The [new] set thus obtained then forms a group of passages through which must pass all narratives and descriptions to come. The group of words [Flaubert has] elaborated is in no way buried as is often the case in Roussel [the novelist Raymond Roussel, one of Ricardou's basic points of reference]. In fact, it immediately signals its presence in a phonetic variation: *charbovari*.

There is one directive that applies to the letter, to construct a given paragraph according to a tendential pangrammaticism of B and C, Bovary's initials. In this context, note the description of the *casquette* [cited previously], which in its association with an idiot's face stands in for Charles. As if by chance, the two groups are each distributed at the beginning and at the end: on the one hand / baleine, boudins, bande / and / broderie, bout, brillait /; on the other hand, / commençait, circulaire / and / cartonné, couvert, compliquée, cordon, croisillon /. What's more: it's enough to associate the first sound of the first word,

OVoïde, with the first sound of the last word, BRIllait, to obtain a BOVRI that is no further off than the hero's own pronunciation.

There is a second directive that applies to an almost [*un à peu près*]: the transition from Charles Bovary to charbovari presupposes the transition from charbovari to charivari, a synonym, as we all know, of pandemonium [*vacarme*]. The text, incidentally, presents us with a proximity that should not surprise us too much. [*"Charbovari. Ce fut un vacarme . . ."*]

A third directive applies a partition between two parts: the end syllable *ry* and the set *Charbova*.

The first clearly indicates where the [sentence] "Toute la classe se mit à rire" comes from. The second, which can easily be read as "char à boeufs" [oxcart] explains on the one hand why Charles is a country boy and on the other why the site of the wedding feast, the place where he gives his name to Emma, is a *charretterie* [a carriage house]. But above all, and this should disturb us, in the opening scene Bovary-the-ox is still young or, if you'd like, he is a *veau* [a calf] or rather a *nouveau* [see the first sentence of the novel, cited above] with a new *casquette*. This makes it possible to understand by means of what phonic relay the opening scene is established: *Bovary*, the young *veau*, fresh from the countryside, is received by a collective character that is much less enigmatic once we note that it brings with it, in the book's very first word, a very opportune syllable: *nous*. (100–02)

For Ricardou, such a "putting in question of the novel by its words" (102) places *Madame Bovary* on the very threshold of literary modernity, at least of the Roussellian stamp.

When Ricardou's essay was published in a volume devoted to the conference, it was accompanied by a transcript of the discussion that had followed his presentation, as was true of the other contributions as well. Not surprisingly, objections to his arguments were raised by various participants. Philippe Bonnefis, for example, pointed out that the production of the "name" BOVRI was problematic as regards "the place in French of the dynamic stress" (103), to which Ricardou countered that as a general rule "one could make room for a conflict between the graphic and the phonic: a given phenomenon might appear on one level and not on the other, and vice-versa" (104). Claudine Gothot-Mersch, the conference organizer, stated flatly that she did not quite believe the BOVRI demonstration (which indeed has not weathered well), adding that for Flaubert "it is the phonic that wins out; just look at the test of the 'gueuloir,' the hunt for alliterations, etc. I also wonder what sense it might make to connect the 'sh' in *Charles*, the 'k' in *cartonné* and the 's' in *circulaire*" (110). She then went on to remark that whereas Ricardou had claimed that Charles was "a country boy because his name is Bovary, that is, ox; I wonder if [Flaubert's] approach is not the inverse: his name would [then] be Bovary because he is a country boy" (110).

Ricardou of course resisted this last suggestion, but then Roger Bismut pointed out that when Charles was a student, "his mother sends the coach to bring his *veau au four* [roast veal]; *veau à la casserole* [braised veal] is served at the wedding feast; when Emma and her husband return from Vaubyessard, they are served *veau à l'oseille* [sorrel veal]. This kind of Vitellization [LAUGHTER] is dominant in agricultural cooperatives. The name of the mayor of Yonville is Tuvache [you cow], and Léon will marry Miss Leboeuf [the ox]. Let me add that the name of the painter who accompanies Charles to choose a tombstone is Vaufrylard. And in her edition, Claudine Gothot-Mersch points out that Flaubert had had that nickname [that is, it was a name taken by Flaubert in his youthful dealings with his friends] such that there is a sort of reverberation of *veau* on himself" (114). (The same network of observations was elaborated with finesse by Jonathan Culler in his 1981 article, "The Uses of *Madame Bovary*," culminating in the observation that "where we expect the real, we get more veal.")[19]

Interestingly, almost nothing was said in discussion about Ricardou's "*charbovari*"–"charivari"–"vacarme" association, which in some ways was the most intriguing of all his proposals. Certainly it has proved remarkably successful, leading even to the writing of a highly original study by Jean-Marie Privat, which reads various cruxes in the novel through an ethnological lens.[20] But presumably it was on participants' minds when they continued to press Ricardou as to whether or not he understood Flaubert to have been conscious of the structures he, Ricardou, claimed to have brought to light. In response, Ricardou insisted that the question of intention, of consciousness, was of no interest to him. "[T]he product interests me only as the effect of a process. Whether the process is conscious or not is not decisive for this process. Thus, a phenomenon that is provoked consciously may now be more visible, now be more concealed, as Roussel's procedure shows, which is at the same time *conscious* and *hidden*" (116–17; emphasis in original). This too did not altogether satisfy his listeners, as Françoise Gaillard made clear toward the end of the discussion, insisting that the "anagrammatical work . . . nevertheless raises a question that you, it seems to me, side-stepped when you brought up the name of Freud [as Ricardou had done earlier] as the name of a kind of guarantor who would allow us to play, but [brought it up] without going all the way with this evocation, that is, all the way to the logic of the unconscious. Because if there is anagrammatical play, the problem becomes, from where is the play regulated, where is the law declared according to which it will be played? What theory of the subject is implied in bringing the anagrammatical play to light?" (120–21) Ricardou responded that he favored the idea of a "'general' unconscious" on the grounds that "word play tends to exceed all restrictions marked by overdetermination according to any prior (ideological or Freudian) formation" (123). Thus the text "on the one hand falls into the jurisdiction of a Freudian analysis or an ideological analysis; on the other, the text is always capable of going beyond them" (122). (In a subsequent book, *Nouveaux problèmes du roman*, Ricardou reviews the discussion following his paper and suggests that "there is a consonance that is *wild* and unconscious in that it takes place, if one can say that, for itself, outside the unconscious intention of the operator.")[21]

2

A brief pause to take stock: I began this essay by documenting (from the *Correspondance*) the aspect of Flaubert's stylistic perfectionism concerning the elimination of unwanted assonances, consonances, and repetitions, before introducing a short passage from the first chapter of *Madame Bovary* littered with the letter *p*. I raised the question as to what we are to make of this, and went on to cite other cruxes in chapter one in which something strange or untoward – something incompatible with an ideal of stylistic seamlessness – has been recognized to occur. This quickly led to extensive quotations from Ricardou's contribution to the 1974 conference as well as from the discussion following his presentation. What I hope has emerged is, first, that by the end of chapter one of *Madame Bovary* attentive readers will have been put on their mettle in the sense of being compelled to come to terms, in one way or another, with an array of unusual textual / linguistic phenomena. Here let me mention in passing that chapter one also contains the first instances in the novel of *style indirect libre* (free indirect style), one of Flaubert's signature narrative resources; of his distinctive employment of the imperfect tense, brilliantly analyzed by Marcel Proust in "A propos du 'style' de Flaubert" of 1920 (about which more shortly); and of the setting of various words in italics, starting with the word *"nouveau"* in the first sentence – an example, it is worth noting, of the primacy of the graphic over the sonic. And second, that coming to terms with those phenomena will necessarily engage, sooner or later, with the question of the author's intentions, or to put this slightly differently, with that of the mode of production of the phenomena under scrutiny. As we have seen, Ricardou wished to minimize that question in favor of directing attention to the phenomena themselves, apart from any consideration of how they came to be produced. But of course so circumscribed a position could not be sustained, especially in view of the fact that at least one set of phenomena he cited, called by Culler Flaubert's "vealism," could only have been intentional on the author's part. (Significantly, as Culler notes, the artist Vaufrylard – one of Flaubert's sobriquets earlier in life, as already noted – who accompanies Charles after Emma's death to help choose a funerary monument, is said to make repeated "calembours," plays on words, a further indication of what is going on.)

This is also true, *a fortiori*, of Flaubert's use of *style indirect libre*, the imperfect, and italics. And just recently a young German scholar, Edi Zollinger, brought out an important monograph in which he demonstrates, or at the very least presents compelling evidence for the view, that Victor Hugo's *Notre-Dame de Paris* forms a major subtext for *Madame Bovary* both in terms of overall design and with regard to specific characters and incidents.[22] So for example Zollinger points to what he takes to be a phonemic affinity between the two novels' respective titles, *maDAME bovARY, notre DAME de pARIS*; he notes the fact that the last sentence spoken by Charles in the former, "C'est la faute de la fatalité!" (500) ["It is the fault of fate!"] has its equivalent in the Greek word ΑΝΑΓΚΗ, meaning fate, which we are told in the preface to Hugo's novel the author found engraved in a dark niche in one of the towers of Notre Dame and which we are later shown being carved there by Claude Frollo, the priest eventually responsible for the death of Esmeralda ("C'est sur ce mot qu'on a fait ce livre," the Preface concludes ["It is on the basis of that word that this book was made"]); the names Frollo and Rodolphe, Zollinger further notes, have much in common lexically, which he understands as linking them thematically as well (Rodolphe, too, deploys the notion of "fatalité" in his letter to Emma breaking off their relationship); he compares the characterization of Charles's "casquette" – "dont la laideur muette a des profondeurs d'expression comme le visage d'un imbécile" – with Hugo's lengthy description of Quasimodo's face, and associates the initial scene in the classroom with the mad laughter that greeted Quasimodo's stating of his name in his courtroom interview with Maître Florian; he points out that Emma calls her dog Djali, which of course is the name of Esmeralda's pet goat in Hugo's novel; and that Esmeralda undergoes the torturing of her delicate foot, an incident which has a later parallel in the sufferings of the clubfoot Hippolyte at the hands of Charles and, indirectly, of Homais; and so on. Following the lead of an article by A. M. Lowe,[23] Zollinger also directs attention to the importance of the Arachne myth in both novels, a connection that enables him to make thematic sense out of Emma's drawing of the head of Minerva, Arachne's rival and nemesis. His larger claim is that at work throughout Flaubert's novel is a fine-grained competition with Hugo's masterpiece of 1831 in the course of which "Arachne (Flaubert) finally takes her revenge for the insult suffered in the punishment imposed by Minerva (Hugo)" (Luzius Keller, in a helpful review of Zollinger's book).[24] In all this there is less emphasis on sheerly verbal associations than one might have expected, though Zollinger makes much of the similarity in sound between the French words "angles" and "gland," the second of which he wants to associate with certain sexual aspects (as he regards them) of Charles's problematic "casquette," and further suggests that the eventual amputation of Hippolyte's leg following Charles's unsuccessful attempt to heal his clubfoot is anticipated earlier in the novel when Mme Lefrançois refers to the former as "Polyte," eliding – in effect amputating – the first syllable of his name. It is still early to assess the larger significance of Zollinger's original and meticulous study, but from the point of view of the present essay the crucial point is that almost all the connections he points to can only have been specifically intended as such by Flaubert.

Two other cruxes in major essays on Flaubert are worth noting in this connection. In Jean Starobinski's justly admired "L'Echelle des températures. Lecture du corps dans *Madame Bovary*,"[25] the critic early on draws attention to a key paragraph in the third chapter of part one. Charles and Emma are in the kitchen of the Rouault house; she has just tilted her head back and licked with her tongue the last traces of curaçao at the bottom of her glass. Then we read:

> Elle se rassit et elle reprit son ouvrage, qui était un bas de coton blanc où elle faisait des reprises; elle travaillait le front baissé; elle ne parlait pas, Charles non plus. L'air, passant par le dessous de la porte, poussait un peu de poussière sur les dalles; il la regardait se traîner, et il entendait seulement le battement intérieur de sa tête, avec le cri d'une poule, au loin, qui pondait dans les cours. Emma, de temps à autre, se rafraîchissait les joues en y appliquant la paume des ses mains, qu'elle refroidissait après cela sur la pomme de fer des grands chenets. (81)

She sat down again and resumed her work – she was darning a white cotton stocking. She sewed with her head bowed, and she did not speak: nor did Charles. A draft was coming in under the door and blowing a little dust across the stone floor; he watched it drift, and was aware of a pulsating sound inside his head – that, and the clucking of a laying hen outside in the yard. From time to time Emma cooled her cheeks with the palms of her hands, and then cooled her hands against the iron knobs of the tall andirons. (25–6)

Starobinski's interest in the passage centers on the theme of bodily perception, in this instance Charles's response to finding himself in Emma's presence, in particular the sentence fragment "et il entendait seulement le battement intérieur de sa tête," and its position in the larger sentence of which it is a part. Starobinski remarks:

The phonic point of view singularly reinforces the structure just discerned. In the section in which the cenesethetic [synesthetic] dominates we find an accumulation of nasal sounds and *t*s: "il *ent*endait seule*ment* le ba*tt*e*ment* in*t*érieur de sa tête." Flaubert carefully avoided assonances: he rightly retained seule*ment* and ba*tt*ement, separated by the slight definite article. In turn, in an approximate symmetry, the beginning and the end of the sentence abound in alliterations, in words beginning with *p* (passant, poussait, poussière, poule, pondait), along with the casually regular rhythm of [u]s (dess*ous*, p*ous*sait, p*ous*sière, p*ou*le, c*ou*rs) and [r]s (ai*r*, po*r*te, poussiè*r*e, *r*egardait, traî*r*er, c*r*i, cou*r*s). Nonetheless, there is a phonic connection between the words that name the things of the outside world and the one that signifies the internal sensation: the (bilabial) *b* of battement is akin to the *p* of *poussière* or of *poule*, from which it differs only in being voiced – which thanks to an associated vibration of the vocal cords, opportunely, *interiorizes* the consonant. (46–7; emphasis in original)

Further on Starobinski comments on the "sensation of a thermic kind" (one of his concerns in the essay) conveyed by Emma's gesture of cooling her cheeks with her palms:

The palm that cools the cheek; then the "*paume*" that cools at the touch of the "*pomme de fer*": the series of perceptions contains two successive contacts, but what is important is not only the alternation of the contact sought by the hand, first with its own body (the cheeks), then with the metallic mass – [what is important] is the thermic gradation, the transition from hot to cold. (50)

The second well-known essay I want to cite, Claude Duchet's "Roman et objets: l'exemple de *Madame Bovary*,"[26] pairs the passage we have just glanced at with an earlier one, also in the Rouault kitchen, marked, Duchet says, by the luxuriance of its verbal matter. Flaubert: "Le déjeuner des gens bouillonnait alentour, dans des petits pots de taille inégale. Des vêtements humides séchaient dans l'intérieur de la cheminée. La pelle, les pincettes et le bec du soufflet, tous de proportion colossale, brillaient comme de l'acier poli, tandis que le long des murs s'étendait une abondante batterie de cuisine, où miroitait inégalement la flamme claire du foyer, jointe aux premières lueurs du soleil arrivant par les carreaux." (71) ["Around its edges the farm hands' breakfast was bubbling in small pots of assorted sizes. Damp clothes were drying inside the vast chimney-opening. The fire shovel, the tongs, and the nose of the bellows, all of colossal proportions, shone like polished steel; and along the walls hung a lavish array of kitchen utensils, glimmering in the bright light of the fire and in the first rays of the sun that were now beginning to come in through the window-panes." (16–17)] And Duchet's commentary:

Note . . . in the first text a redundancy, an exuberance of the verbal matter: repetition of *p*s, echoed phonemes (*abondante batte*rie), a succession of open *e*s (la *pelles, les pincettes et le bec du soufflet*: an association by contiguity that metonymically signifies the chimney and connotes the gaiety of the flame and the reassuring values of the home). If we restore to the word-objects their surroundings, the end of the sequence is nothing but a moving surface of light onto which two groups of objects throw their reflections; the small pots of *inégale* [unequal] size are themselves integrated by the adverb *inégalement* [unequally] into the syntagm of brilliance and dance. In fact, nothing happens: everything is shot through with light, bursting with life in a familiar, even a family calmness. (35)

Duchet continues:

> In the other sequence [the one beginning "Elle se rassit . . ."] [we find] on the contrary a certain silence of the word-objects, immobile witnesses to a history that unfolds outside of them, a history on which they weigh nonetheless. This is confirmed by a remarkable exception we come across in our reading: Emma cooled the *paume* of her hand on the *pomme de fer* of the great andirons. Flaubert comes to the opposition p*aume* and p*omme* at the last moment: it does not exist in earlier versions. The object, too, lends itself to such play, to such encounters with human beings. Assonance and dissonance here are like a limping of the text and cause discomfort. The key to this verbal trap is perhaps, cruelly, to be found somewhere else: think of the young beaux at the theater with their "cravate vert-pomme" [actually the novel says "cravate rose ou vert pomme"], "appuyant sur des badines à pomme d'or la paume tendue de leurs gants jaunes" [Flaubert, *Madame Bovary*, 341]. A ballet of objects . . . , a mechanics of derision! "Calculation and tricks of style!" [The sentence in quotation marks is a seemingly ironic quotation of a derisive judgment of Leconte de Lisle's *Les Poèmes antiques* in a letter from Flaubert to Louise Colet.] (35–6)

Slightly further on Duchet writes:

> We could cite other examples of linked syntagmata in which objects generate one another through a series of transformations of their phonic substances without for all that becoming redundant in the formal play of alliterations and paronomasia. When Emma imagines the world of the ambassadors [in a passage cited below] she sees "tables ovales couvertes d'un tapis de velours à crépines d'or" ["oval tables covered with gold-fringed velvet"]. The table's "*ovale*" (form-meaning, a connotation of luxury), leads to "*velours*," relayed by "*couvertes*"; "*tapis*" takes up "*table*" and announces "*crépines*," which erupts as the dream rears up one last time. (36)

What is striking, to my mind, is not only that both Starobinski and Duchet single out for analysis passages marked by alliteration, assonance, and repetition but also that they are content for the most part to leave it not quite clear whether or not they consider those effects to have been consciously intended by the author. Or perhaps I should say consciously intended *as such*, since both critics would likely claim that the relationships they highlight were part of the manifestly intentional enterprise of writing *Madame Bovary*. This is doubtless true – but what of, for example, Duchet's claim that the "key" to the "verbal trap" represented for him by the near-repetition "paume" / "pomme" in the "Elle se rassit . . ." passage lies in the considerably later reference to the young dandies and their gloves? Duchet's quotation from Flaubert's letter to Colet ("Calcul et ruses du style!") implies that he takes that set of relationships to have been a deliberate construction on Flaubert's part. But to what end? And is that really plausible? In any case, the other instances of phonemic play to which he draws attention and which he associates with the novel's structuration by what he calls "paradigmatic" and "syntagmatic" series of similar objects remain unspecified with respect to the nature of the authorial activity that gave rise to them in the first place.

Consider another paragraph featuring Emma from part one of the novel. By now Charles is making regular visits to the Rouault farm to check on his patient, Emma's father, but of course what keeps drawing him there is the prospect of seeing Emma (we are told that he doesn't quite realize this). The close of one visit is narrated as follows:

> Elle le reconduisait toujours jusqu'à la première marche du perron. Lorsqu'on n'avait pas encore amené son cheval, elle restait là. On s'était dit adieu, on ne parlait plus; le grand air l'entourait, levant pêle-mêle les petits cheveux follets de sa nuque, ou secouant sur sa hanche les cordons de son tablier, qui se tortillaient comme des banderoles. Une fois, par un temps de dégel, l'écorce des arbres suintait dans la cour, la neige sur les couvertures des bâtiments se fondait. Elle était sur le seuil; elle alla chercher son ombrelle, elle l'ouvrit. L'ombrelle, de soie gorge de pigeon, que traversait le soleil, éclairait de reflets mobiles la peau

blanche de sa figure. Elle souriait là-dessous à la chaleur tiède; on entendait les gouttes d'eau, une à une, tomber sur la moire tendue. (75)

She always accompanied him to the foot of the steps outside the door. If his horse hadn't been brought around she would wait there with him. At such moments they had already said good-bye, and stood there silent; the breeze eddied around her, swirling the stray wisps of hair at her neck, or sending her apron strings flying like streamers around her waist. Once she was standing there on a day of thaw, when the bark of the trees in the farmyard was oozing sap and the snow was melting on the roofs. She went inside for her parasol, and opened it. The parasol was of rosy iridescent silk, and the sun pouring through it painted the white skin of her face with flickering patches of light. Beneath it she smiled at the springlike warmth; and drops of water could be heard falling one by one on the taut moiré. (20)

It would be hard to overstate the sheer beauty of this paragraph as a specimen of Flaubert's prose at its most seductive, or indeed its extraordinary power of sensuous evocation, which Jacques Neefs has sought to capture in his fine essay, "'Du réel écrit . . .'."[27] Neefs writes: "It is precisely the 'rabid detail' ["détail enragé," a phrase of Barbey d'Aurevilly, used in deprecation of Flaubert's descriptions in *Madame Bovary*] that Flaubert's prose seeks to render active, present, persisting in the reader's memory. The visibility constructed by the prose must *insist*. In a tableau like that of Emma 'on the threshold' of the Bertaux farm, a new experience of the sensible is at stake, in its mobile multiplicity, in the apprehension the tableau gives us of a figure in space" (700; emphasis in original). Neefs goes on to remark, altogether persuasively, that to think of such a description of Emma as "focalized" by Charles's perceptions is completely insufficient; "that is like a reduction that would restore to another subject (albeit to a fictive and rather frail one) the responsibility for what remains persistently in sight." Rather: "There is in the writing itself a desire to see, to feel, to preserve the image, which is of the order of the tension that is active in the seeing of a painting" (701). (Neefs had earlier compared the description of Emma to modern French painting "en plein air.") There is more in this vein – also fine discussions of other passages – culminating in the statement that moments such as those he has been analyzing "demand a kind of assent to the fiction, assent to its sensible, rhythmic, profound detail. . . . If *Madame Bovary* has excited such fascination, along with [a counter-feeling of] rejection provoked by the disruption of sight and perspectives – and, for that reason, of 'moral' perspectives – it is because the novel implied a mental and sensible participation of an entirely new kind" (707).

I think this is acute, and would add that this new type of mental and sensible participation also involves, at least ideally – I am, of course, speaking for myself, but with a view to a wider representativeness (more on this shortly) – a heightened recognition of the play of syllables and phonemes, which is to say of assonances (recon*d*uisait, perr*on*, *on*, *en*core, s*on*, *On*, *on*, gr*an*d, l'*en*tourait, lev*an*t, secou*an*t, h*an*che, cord*on*s, banderoles, etc.), alliteration (*p*remière, *p*erron, *p*arlait, *p*lus, *p*êle-mêle, *p*etits . . . also l'en*t*ourait, *p*etits, *t*ablier, *t*ortillait, *t*emps, suin*t*ait, couver*t*ures, bâ*t*iments, é*t*ait, *t*raversait, *t*iède, en*t*endait, gou*t*tes, *t*omber, *t*endue), as well as, starting halfway through the paragraph, of a persistent repetition or indeed *rhyme* that quickly comes to seem emblematic of an obsessional thread running through the paragraph as a whole (*elle*, *elle*, ombr*elle*, *elle*, l'ombr*elle*, *elle*, shadowed or refracted by pê*l*e-mê*l*e, fo*ll*ets, torti*ll*aient, bander*ol*es, dég*el*, *al*la, s*ol*eil, éc*l*airait, ref*l*ets, mobi*l*es, cha*l*eur).

Nor does this last tendency cease with the end of the paragraph. The next paragraph reads:

> Dans les premiers temps que Charles fréquentait les Bertaux, madame Bovary jeune ne manquait pas de s'informer du malade, et même sur le livre qu'elle tenait en partie double, elle avait chosi pour M. Rouault une belle page blanche. Mais quand elle sut qu'il avait une fille, elle alla aux informations; et elle apprit que mademoiselle Rouault, élevée au couvent, chez les Ursulines, avait reçu, comme on dit, *une belle éducation*, qu'elle savait, en conséquence, la danse, la géographie, le dessin, faire de la tapisserie et toucher du piano. Ce fut le comble! (75; emphasis in original)

During the first period of Charles's visits to Les Berteaux, Madame Bovary never failed to ask about the patient's progress; and in her double-entry ledger she had given Monsieur Rouault a fine new page to himself. But when she heard that he had a daughter she began to make inquiries; and she learned that Mademoiselle Rouault had had her schooling in a convent, with the Ursuline nuns – had received, as the saying went, a "fine education," in the course of which she had been taught dancing, geography, drawing, needlework and a little piano. Think of that! (20)

Note, by the way, how in the second paragraph the word "elle," after having been dedicated to Emma and her "ombrelle" in the first, mainly refers to Charles's wife, until in the penultimate sentence the last of six "elle"s returns to Emma – a perfect example of the sort of ambiguity with respect to personal pronouns that Proust will single out in his great essay of 1920 as a characteristic of Flaubert's prose, where it is associated with the latter's pursuit of a "hermetic continuity of style."[28] This is doubtless true, though it is also worth remarking on the tiny hitch in one's reading – in the continuity of one's absorption in the text – that the sixth "elle," coming right after *"une belle éducation,"* inevitably causes. (An earlier hitch, of course, is caused by what can only feel like the hijacking of "elle" away from Emma in the first place.)*

* Just to show how far even the most devotedly rigorous English translation necessarily departs from the phonemic structure of the French, here are the two paragraphs as rendered by Lydia Davis in 2010:

She would always see him out as far as the foot of the front steps. When his horse had not yet been brought around, she would stay there. They had said goodbye, they did not go on talking; the fresh air surrounded her, lifting in disarray the stray wisps of hair on the nape of her neck or tossing her apron strings so that they snaked like banners about her hips. Once, during a thaw, the bark of the trees was oozing in the yard, the snow on the tops of the buildings was melting. She was on the doorsill; she went to get her parasol, she opened it. The parasol, of dove-gray iridescent silk, with the sun shining through it, cast moving glimmers of light over the white skin of her face. She was smiling beneath it in the mild warmth; and they could hear the drops of water, one be one, falling on the taut moiré.

3

My question, as before, is what to make of all this. Certainly the internal word-to-word, syllable-to-syllable, phoneme-to-phoneme relationships I have just highlighted in the two paragraphs in question – one a textbook example of Flaubert's style at its most exalted – are not, or at least are not obviously, compatible with notions such as his reputed, indeed self-declared, "chasse aux assonances" (and "consonances"). And yet if Flaubert is to be believed, and there is not the slightest reason to doubt him, each of the above sentences is likely to have passed through the ordeal of the "gueuloir," almost certainly on several occasions. I find this puzzling. Indeed I admit to being somewhat puzzled why previous commentators have not called attention to those relationships as a problem for criticism – or to put this slightly differently, why I have always found them so conspicuous and thought-provoking whereas others, it would seem, have not.

One likely answer to the second way of framing the question is that this has almost everything to do with my personal distance from the French language. That is, although I studied French in high school and college, and have lived in Paris for weeks and months at a stretch, and have read intensively in the work of French writers and thinkers since my early twenties, and have spent much of my intellectual career closely engaged with eighteenth- and nineteenth-century French painting and art

---

During the early days of Charles's visits to Les Bertaux, Madame Bovary the younger never failed to ask after the patient, and she had even in the double-columned book she kept, chosen for Monsieur Rouault a nice blank page. But when she found out that he had a daughter, she made inquiries; and she learned that Mademoiselle Rouault, raised in a convent, among the Ursulines, had received, as they say, *a fine education*, that she knew, consequently, dancing, geography, drawing, how to do tapestry work and play the piano. That was the limit! (Gustave Flaubert, *Madame Bovary: Provincial Ways*, trans. Lydia Davis (New York and London, 2010), 15–16.)

The difference between the original and the translation is all the more striking in that Davis seems deliberately to have courted internal rhymes and similar relationships, no doubt in an attempt to capture something of the phonemic play of the original.

criticism, and have enjoyed gratifying friendships with French men and women in scholarship and the arts, my facility in French remains, sadly, limited. Without going into embarrassing detail, I will simply say that the French language is for me not an atmosphere I unreflectingly breathe nor an ocean in which I confidently swim. But precisely because this is so, precisely because my inner "ear" and reading "eye" remain unhabituated to the ordinary mellifluous and unimpeded flow of French speech and writing, I sometimes have the sense of being struck – sonically and visually – by certain quasi-material features of a particular text or passage that a native or native-quality speaker/reader might well not (indeed almost certainly would not) pause over but that are not on that account, I want to claim, completely without importance. With respect to *Madame Bovary*, a work I read in French for the first time in my twenties and have returned to on a dozen subsequent occasions, I have always regarded it as, in the words of Vladimir Dmitrievich Nabokov – the novelist's father – "the unsurpassed pearl of French literature" (a judgment with which the son concurred),[29] largely on the strength of the extraordinary textual "activity" of the sort that I have been doing my best to bring to light. I take it to be an open question as to how most accurately to characterize the effect of such "activity" on the reader. In the two paragraphs we have just examined, for example, despite my mention of a slight "hitch" or two in my absorption in the text owing to the play of "elle"s, the cumulative effect is not at all that of a conflict between different textual "directives," as in Ricardou's account of various cruxes in chapter one. (His general rubric of "Belligérance du texte" does not feel apt to me in the least.) Rather, my sense is of attending simultaneously, one might say fugally, to multiple registers – at the very least that of the narrative import of the whole; the inspired description of persons, accessories, and environments (the entire "construction of visibility" on which Neefs insists); the idiosyncrasies of grammar and syntax, and beyond those the rhythmic flow, the "hermetic" continuity, of the sentences; and by no means least of all, the ceaseless, constantly changing, wholly unpredictable play of assonances, consonances, rhymes, off-rhymes, and repetitions of all sorts such as I have just canvassed – all framed, given an "ontological" cast, by Flaubert's authorial ideal of an overarching impersonality (more on which shortly) – without any of those registers actively interfering other than extremely fleetingly with any of the others (like a dissonance in music that is quickly resolved or otherwise got past). In other words, my sense is of a general, and at certain moments "ecstatic" heightening or intensification of the act of reading, as if indeed, adapting Jacques Neefs, *Madame Bovary* both calls for and rewards a new sort of readerly participation in the inward "activation" (I do not quite wish to say "production") of the text, less a condition of total absorption or immersion (of self-forgetting) than one in which several different modes of awareness are present simultaneously to the reader's mind (and ear, and eye), in consequence of which the reader comes to experience almost a sense of "identification," if not with the act of writing as such at any rate with the text's seeming capacity to continuously – which is to say in sentence after sentence, paragraph after paragraph (the basic unit of Flaubert's prose)[30] – provide further compelling instances of its own special mode of literariness (of eliciting literary interest, to kidnap a term of Steven Knapp's[31]). Presumably all sensitive native or native-quality readers of *Madame Bovary* have had some version of this experience, but presumably also it has seemed so natural and absorbing to them as not to call for explicit comment.[32]

But this too – this way of phrasing the matter – raises the question of Flaubert's relation to the effects I have been trying to evoke. Sometimes, even often, the nature of those effects is such as to indicate the priority of authorial agency down to the smallest unit of the prose. For example, in one memorable paragraph in the "Comices" chapter (part II, chapter 8), the farm animals at the fair are described in terms that almost oppressively evoke a sense of unqualified, not to say compounded, physicality. Thus we read:

> Les bêtes étaient là, le nez tourné vers la ficelle, et alignant confusément leurs croupes inégales. [An amazing sentence – but wait.] Des porcs assoupis enfonçaient en terre leur groin; des veaux

beuglaient; des brebis bêlaient; les vaches, un jarret replié, étalaient leur
ventre sur le gazon, et, ruminant lentement, clignaient leurs paupières
lourdes, sous les moucherons qui bourdonnaient autour d'elles. Des
charretiers, les bras nus, retenaient par le licou des étalons cabrés, qui
hennissaient à pleins naseaux du côté des juments. Elles restaient pais-
ibles, allongeant la tête et la crinière pendante, tandis que leurs poulains
se reposaient à leur ombre, ou venaient les téter quelquefois; et, sur la
longue ondulation de tous ces corps tassés, on voyait se lever au vent,
comme un flot, quelque crinière blanche, ou bien saillir des cornes
aiguës, et des têtes d'hommes qui couraient. A l'écart, en dehors des
lices, cent pas plus loin, il y avait un grand taureau noir muselé, portant
un cercle de fer à la narine, et qui ne bougeait pas plus qu'une bête de
bronze. Un enfant en haillons le tenait par une corde. (234)

Here stood the livestock, noses to the rope, rumps of all shapes and
sizes forming a ragged line. Lethargic pigs were nuzzling the earth with
their snouts; calves were lowing and sheep bleating; cows with their
legs folded under them lay on the grass, slowly chewing their cud and
blinking their heavy eyelids under the midges buzzing around them.
Barc-armed teamsters were holding rearing stallions by the halter:
these were neighing loudly in the direction of the mares, who stood
there quietly, necks outstretched and manes drooping, as their foals
rested in their shadow or came now and again to suck. Above the long
undulating line of these massed bodies a white mane would occasionally surge up like a wave in the wind, or a pair of sharp horns would
stick out, or men's heads would bob up as they ran. Quite apart, outside
the arena, a hundred yards off, was a big black bull with a strap harness
and an iron ring through its nose, motionless as a brazen image. A
ragged little boy held it by a rope. (154–5)

In this instance it would be pointless to italicize assonances, alliterations,
similar phonemes, and the like; the entire paragraph – six sentences long
– is a dense, almost impassable forest of sonic (also graphic) material that
almost might be said to resist being read. In any case, the reader has to
make a distinct effort of a special sort – a new sort – to read it through

(almost to trudge through it) from beginning to end. Typically, though, of Flaubert, supreme master of paragraphing, the last, short sentence strikes a sharply different, crisply visual note – "Un enfant en haillons le tenait par une corde." – which of course only intensifies the impression of deliberate, not to say laborious construction produced by the paragraph as a whole. (A suggestion: the set apart "grand taureau noir muselé" is Flaubert, or rather one of his several incarnations in the novel. In other words, he is no ordinary "veau." And a further thought: Flaubert's term of endearment for Colet throughout his correspondence with her was "chère Muse"; the unexpected epithet "muselé" would then be another of the novel's "calembours," intended as such or otherwise. Which is it though? You see how hard it is to achieve clarity here.)

But what of the following, the first paragraph in part I, chapter 4, narrating the arrival of guests at Charles and Emma's wedding:

> Les conviés arrivèrent de bonne heure dans des voitures, carrioles à un cheval, chars à bancs à deux roues, vieux cabriolets sans capote, tapissières à rideaux de cuir, et les jeunes gens des villages les plus voisins dans des charrettes où ils se tenaient debout, en rang, les mains appuyées sur les ridelles pour ne pas tomber, allant au trot et secoués dur. Il en vint de dix lieues loin, de Goderville, de Normanville et de Cany. On avait invité tous les parents des deux familles, on s'était raccommodé avec les amis brouillés, on avait écrit à des connaissances perdues de vue depuis longtemps. (85)

> The invited guests arrived early in a variety of vehicles – one-horse shays, two-wheeled charabancs, old gigs without tops, vans with leather curtains; and the young men from the nearest villages came in farm-carts, standing one behind the other along the sides and grasping the rails to keep from being thrown, for the horses trotted briskly and the roads were rough. They came from as far as twenty-five miles away, from Goderville, from Normanville, from Cany. All the relations of both families had been asked, old quarrels had been patched up, letters sent to acquaintances long lost sight of. (29)

I take it that by now the sheer density of alliteration based on the letters (hard) *c*, *v*, *p*, *d*, and *t* (and perhaps also *l*) does not require detailed commentary. Once more the question is what to make of this – in particular whether we are to understand that alliteration as having been in all cases fully intended by Flaubert (bracketing for the moment the question of what full intention might mean in this context) or whether at least some of those repetitions are the result of automatisms of one sort or another – whether despite having survived the grill of the "gueuloir," the alliterations somehow escaped the writer's notice. (If that is not the case, why would he have allowed them to survive into the final text?)

Some further examples seem called for in order to prove beyond a doubt that those we have looked at are not exceptional in this regard. My problem is how best to choose from a wealth of possibilities; here are fifteen, selected not quite haphazardly, in the order they occur in the novel.*

(1) First, just two sentences from the description of the approach to Yonville-l'Abbaye from the beginning of part II of the novel:

> Les toits de chaume, comme les bonnets de fourrure rabattus sur des yeux, descendent jusqu'au tiers à peu près des fenêtres basses, dont les gros verres bombés sont garnis d'un noeud dans le milieu, à la façon des culs de bouteilles. Sur le mur de plâtre que traversent en diagonale des lambourdes noires, s'accroche parfois quelque maigre poirier, et les rez-de-chaussée ont à leur porte une petite barrière tournante pour les défendre des poussins, qui viennent picorer, sur le seuil, des miettes de pain bis trempé de cidre. (146–7)[33]

---

* Naturally, I am aware that in the course of the following pages the reader may come to feel that the same general point might have been made more economically, on the strength of fewer examples. No doubt this is true. But my project in this essay requires a certain force of demonstration, which in turn depends on the reader being persuaded that I am not basing my rather extravagant claims on just a handful of unrepresentative citations. The precise nature of those claims will become clear only further on, with the introduction of certain considerations bearing on the issue of habit, *l'habitude*.

The thatched roofs hide the top third or so of the low windows like fur caps pulled down over eyes, and each windowpane, thick and convex, has a bull's-eye in its center like the bottom of a bottle. Some of the plastered house walls with their diagonal black timbers are the background for scraggly espaliered pear trees; and the house doors have little swinging gates to keep out the baby chicks, who come to the sill to peck at brown-bread crumbs soaked in cider. (81)

(2) Second, a longish citation, Emma after the ball at Vaubyessard fantasizing about Paris:

Elle étudia, dans Eugène Sue, des descriptions d'ameublements; elle lut Balzac et George Sand, y cherchant des assouvissements imaginaires pour ses convoitises personelles. A table même, elle apportait son livre, et elle tournait les feuillets, pendant que Charles mangeait en lui parlant. Le souvenir du Vicomte revenait toujours dans ses lectures. Entre lui et les personnages inventés, elle établissait des rapprochements. Mais le cercle dont il était le centre peu à peu s'élargit autour de lui, et cette auréole qu'il avait, s'écartant de sa figure, s'étala plus au loin, pour illuminer d'autres rêves.

Paris, plus vague que l'Océan, miroitait donc aux yeux d'Emma dans une atmosphère vermeille. La vie nombreuse qui s'agitait en ce tumulte y était cependant divisée par parties, classée en tableaux distincts. Emma n'en apercevait que deux ou trois qui lui cachaient tous les autres, et représentaient à eux seuls l'humanité complète. Le monde des ambassadeurs marchait sur des parquets luisants, dans des salons lambrissés de miroirs, autour de tables ovales couvertes d'un tapis de velours à crépines d'or. Il y avait là des robes à queue, de grands mystères, des angoisses dissimulées sous des sourires. Venait ensuite la société des duchesses; on y était pâle; on se levait à quatre heures; les femmes, pauvres anges! portaient du point d'Angleterre au bas de leur jupon, et les hommes, capacités méconnues sous des dehors futiles, crevaient leurs chevaux par partie de plaisir, allaient passer à Bade la saison d'été, et, vers la quarantaine enfin, épousaient des héritières. (128–9)

She pored over the interior decorating details in the novels of Eugène Sue; she read Balzac and George Sand, seeking in their pages vicarious satisfaction for her own desires. She brought her book with her even to meals, and turned the leaves while Charles ate and talked to her. Her readings always brought the vicomte back to her mind: she continually found similarities between him and the fictitious characters. But the circle whose center he was gradually widened; and the halo she had given him spread beyond his image, gilding other dreams.

Paris, city vaster than the ocean, glittered before Emma's eyes in a rosy light. But the teeming life of the tumultuous place was divided into compartments, separated into distinct scenes. Emma was aware of only two or three, which shut out the sight of the others and stood for all mankind. In drawing rooms with mirrored walls and gleaming floors, around oval tables covered with gold-fringed velvet, moved the world of the ambassadors. It was full of trailing gowns, deep secrets, and unbearable tensions concealed beneath smiles. Then came the circle of the duchesses: here everyone was pale and lay in bed till four; the women – poor darlings! – wore English lace on their petticoat hems; and the men, their true worth unsuspected under their frivolous exteriors, rode horses to death for the fun of it, spent their summers at Baden-Baden, and eventually, when they were about forty, married heiresses. (65)

(3) Five or so pages later:

Au fond de son âme, cependant, elle attendait un événement. Comme les matelots en détresse, elle promenait sur la solitude de sa vie des yeux désespérés, cherchant au loin quelque voile blanche dans les brumes de l'horizon. Elle ne savait pas quel serait ce hasard, le vent qui le pousserait jusqu'à elle, vers quel rivage il la mènerait, s'il était chaloupe ou vaisseau à trois ponts, chargé d'angoisses ou plein de félicités jusqu'aux sabords. Mais, chaque matin, à son réveil, elle l'espérait pour la journée, et elle écoutait tous les bruits, se levait en sursaut, s'étonnait qu'il ne vînt pas; puis, au coucher du soleil, toujours plus triste, désirait être au lendemain. (134)

Deep down, all the while, she was waiting for something to happen. Like a sailor in distress, she kept casting desperate glances over the solitary waste of her life, seeking some white sail in the distant mists of the horizon. She had no idea by what wind it would reach her, toward what shore it would bear her, or what kind of craft it would be – tiny boat or towering vessel, laden with heartbreaks or filled to the gunwales with rapture. But every morning when she awoke she hoped that today would be the day; she listened for every sound, gave sudden starts, was surprised when nothing happened; and then, sadder with each succeeding sunset, she longed for tomorrow. (69–70)

(4) And here is the unforgettable tableau of Emma warming herself by the fire in the kitchen of the *Lion d'or* at Yonville shortly after her and Charles's arrival there:

Madame Bovary, quand elle fut dans la cuisine, s'approcha de la cheminée. Du bout de ses deux doigts, elle prit sa robe à la hauteur du genou, et, l'ayant ainsi remontée jusqu'aux chevilles, elle tendit à la flamme, par-dessus le gigot qui tournait, son pied chaussé d'une bottine noire. Le feu l'éclairait en entier, pénétrant d'une lumière crue la trame de sa robe, les pores égaux de sa peau blanche et même les paupières de ses yeux qu'elle clignait de temps à autre. Une grande couleur rouge passait sur elle, selon le souffle du vent qui venait par la porte entrouverte.

De l'autre côté de la cheminée, un jeune homme à chevelure blonde la regardait silencieusement. (159)

In the kitchen, Madame Bovary crossed to the fireplace. Reaching halfway down her skirt, she grasped it with the tips of two of her fingers, raised it to her ankles, and stretched out a black-shod foot toward the flame, over the leg of mutton that was turning on the spit. She was standing in the full light of the fire, and by its harsh glare one could see the weave of her dress, the pores of her white skin, even her eyelids when she briefly shut her eyes. Now and then she was flooded by a great glow of red, as a gust of wind blew into the fire from the half-open kitchen door.

From the other side of the fireplace a fair-haired young man was silently watching her. (90–91)

(5) A particularly charged paragraph relates Lheureux's display of his goods to Emma, whose response for the moment is left largely undefined.

Alors M. Lheureux exhiba délicatement trois écharpes algériennes, plusieurs paquets d'aiguilles anglaises, une paire de pantoufles en paille, et, enfin, quatre coquetiers en coco, ciselés à jour par des forçats. Puis, les deux mains sur la table, le cou tendu, la taille penchée, il suivait, bouche béante, le regard d'Emma, qui se promenait indécis parmi ces marchandises. De temps à autre, comme pour en chasser la poussière, il donnait un coup d'ongle sur la soie des écharpes, dépliées dans toute leur longueur; et elles frémissaient avec un bruit léger, en faisant, à la lumière verdâtre du crépuscule, scintiller, comme de petites étoiles, les paillettes d'or de leur tissu. (191)

Then Monsieur Lheureux daintily held out for her inspection three Algerian scarves, some packages of English needles, a pair of straw slippers, and finally four cocoanut-shell egg cups, carved in an openwork design by convicts. Then, both hands on the table, leaning forward, his neck outstretched, he watched Emma open mouthed, following her gaze as it wandered uncertainly over the merchandise. From time to time, as though to brush off a bit of dust, he gave a flick of a fingernail to the silk of the scarves, lying there unfolded to their full length; and they quivered and rustled under his touch, their gold sequins gleaming like little stars in the greenish light of the dusk. (117)

(6) Emma's state after the departure of Léon for Rouen goes through several phases, of which this is one:

Cependant les flammes s'apaisèrent, soit que la provision d'elle-même s'épuisât, ou que l'entassement fût trop considérable. L'amour, peu à peu, s'éteignit par l'absence, le regret s'étouffa sous l'habitude; et cette lueur d'incendie qui empourprait son ciel pâle se couvrit de plus d'ombre et s'effaça par degrés. Dans l'assoupissement de sa conscience, elle prit même les répugnances du mari pour des aspirations

vers l'amant, les brûlures de la haine pour des réchauffements de la ten-
dresse; mais, comme l'ouragan soufflait toujours, et que la passion se
consuma jusqu'aux cendres, et qu'aucun secours ne vint, qu'aucun
soleil ne parut, il fut de tous côtés nuit complète, et elle demeura
perdue dans un froid horrible qui la traversait. (217)

Nevertheless the flames did die down – whether exhausted from lack
of supplies or choked by excessive feeding. Little by little, love was
quenched by absence; regret was smothered by routine; and the fiery
glow that had reddened her pale sky grew gray and gradually vanished.
In this growing inner twilight she even mistook her recoil from her
husband for an aspiration toward her lover, the searing waves of hatred
for a rekindling of love. But the storm kept raging, her passion burned
itself to ashes, no help was forthcoming, no new sun rose on the
horizon. Night closed in completely around her, and she was left alone
in a horrible void of piercing cold. (140)

(7) In chapter 11 of part II the arrival from Neufchâtel of Dr. Canivet,
who will perform the amputation of Hippolyte's leg, is described as
follows:

Il arriva dans son cabriolet, qu'il conduisait lui-même. Mais, le
ressort du côté droit s'étant à la longue affaissé sous le poids de sa corpulence, il se faisait que la voiture penchait un peu tout en allant, et
l'on apercevait sur l'autre coussin près de lui une vaste boîte, couverte
de basane rouge, dont les trois fermoirs de cuivre brillaient magis-
tralement.[34] (290)

He drove up in his gig, holding the reins himself. Over the years the
right-hand spring had given way under the weight of his corpulence,
so that the carriage sagged a little to one side as it rolled along. Beside
him, on the higher half of the seat cushion, could be seen a huge red
leather case, its three brass clasps gleaming magisterially. (205–6)

(8) Further on, Emma and Charles take the *diligence* to Rouen to attend
the opera, where by chance they will meet Léon:

La diligence descendait à l'hôtel de la *Croix rouge*, sur la place Beauvoisine. C'était une de ces auberges comme il y en a dans tous les faubourgs de province, avec de grandes écuries et de petites chambres à coucher, où l'on voit au milieu de la cour des poules picorant l'avoine sous les cabriolets crottés des commis voyageurs; – bon vieux gîtes à balcon de bois vermoulu qui craquent au vent dans les nuits d'hiver, continuellement pleins de monde, de vacarme et de mangeaille, dont les tables noires sont poissées par les *glorias*, les vitres épaisses jaunies par les mouches, les serviettes humides tachées par le vin bleu; et qui, sentant toujours le village, comme des valets de ferme habillés en bourgeois, ont un café sur la rue, et du côté de la campagne un jardin à légumes. Charles immédiatement se mit en courses. Il confondit l'avant-scène avec les galeries, le *parquet* avec les loges, demanda des explications, ne les comprit pas, fut renvoyé du contrôleur au directeur, revint à l'auberge, retourna au bureau, et, plusieurs fois ainsi, arpenta toute la longueur de la ville, depuis le théâtre jusqu'au boulevard. (338–9)

The coach took them to the Hotel de la Croix-Rouge in the Place Beauvoisine. It was one of those inns such as you find on the edge of every provincial city, with large stables and small bedrooms, and chickens scratching for oats in the coach yard under muddy gigs belonging to traveling salesmen – comfortable, old-fashioned stopovers, with worm-eaten wooden balconies that creak in the wind on winter nights, constantly full of people, bustle and victuals, their blackened table tops sticky with spilled coffee-and-brandies, their thick windowpanes yellowed by flies, their napkins spotted blue by cheap red wine. They always seem a little rustic, like farm hands in Sunday clothes; on the street side they have a café, and in back – on the country side – a vegetable garden. Charles went at once to buy tickets. He got the stage boxes mixed up with the top balconies, and the rest of the boxes with the orchestra; he asked for explanations, didn't understand them, was sent from the box office to the manager, came back to the hotel, went back to the box office again. All in all, between the theater and the outer boulevard he covered the entire length of the city several times. (248–9)

(9) And a page later:

> De peur de paraître ridicule, Emma voulut, avant d'entrer, faire un tour de promenade sur le port, et Bovary, par prudence, garda les billets à sa main, dans la poche de son pantalon, qu'il appuyait contre son ventre.
>
> Un battement de coeur la prit dès le vestibule. Elle sourit involontairement de vanité, en voyant la foule qui se précipitait à droite par l'autre corridor, tandis qu'elle montait l'escalier des *premières*. Elle eut plaisir, comme un enfant, à pousser de son doigt les larges portes tapissées; elle aspira de toute sa poitrine l'odeur poussiéreuse des couloirs, et, quand elle fut assise dans sa loge, elle se cambra la taille avec une désinvolture de duchesse. (340)

> Fearing lest they appear ridiculous, Emma insisted that they stroll a bit along the river front before going in; and Bovary, by way of precaution, kept the tickets in his hand and his hand in his trousers pocket, pressed reassuringly against his stomach.
>
> Her heart began to pound as they entered the foyer. A smile of satisfaction rose involuntarily to her lips at seeing the crowd hurry off to the right down the corridor, while she climbed the stairs leading to the first tier. She took pleasure, like a child, in pushing open the wide upholstered doors with one finger; she filled her lungs with the dusty smell of the corridors; and seated in her box she drew herself up with all the airs of a duchess. (250)

(10) Two other moments in the opera chapter are also striking in this connection. The first occurs when she is fantasizing about Lagardy, the singer:

> Il devait avoir, pensait-elle, un intarissable amour, pour en déverser sur la foule à si larges effluves. Toutes ses velléités de dénigrement s'évanouissaient sous la poésie du rôle qui l'envahissait, et, entraînée

vers l'homme par l'illusion du personnage, elle tâcha de se figurer sa vie, cette vie retentissante, extraordinaire, splendide, et qu'elle aurait pu mener cependant, si le hasard l'avait voulu. (345)

His love, she thought, must be inexhaustible, since he could pour it out in such great quantities on the crowd. Her resolution not to be taken in by the display of false sentiment was swept away by the impact of the singer's eloquence [the translation gets a bit loose here]; the fiction he was embodying drew her to his real life, and she tried to imagine what it was like – that glamorous, fabulous, marvelous life that she, too, might have lived had chance so willed it. (254)

And slightly later:

L'odeur du gaz se mêlait aux haleines; le vent des éventails rendait l'atmosphère plus étouffante. Emma voulut sortir; la foule encombrait les corridors, et elle retomba dans son fauteuil avec des palpitations qui la suffoquaient. Charles, ayant peur de la voir s'évanouir, courut à la buvette lui chercher un verre d'orgeat. (346)

The smell of the gas mingled with human exhalations, and the air seemed the more stifling for being stirred up by fans. Emma tried to get out, but there was a crush in the corridors, and she sank back onto a chair, oppressed by palpitations. Charles, fearful lest she fall into a faint, hurried to the bar for a glass of orgeat. (255)

(11) Leap ahead to the famous paragraph describing the first view of Rouen as seen every Thursday morning by Emma from *l'Hirondelle* as she hastened to Léon. The paragraph preceding the one in question ends with the sentence, "Puis, d'un seul coup d'oeil, la ville apparaissait." Then:

Descendant tout en amphithéâtre et noyée dans le brouillard, elle s'élargissait au-delà des ponts, confusément. La pleine campagne remontait ensuite d'un mouvement monotone, jusqu'à toucher au loin la base indécise du ciel pâle. Ainsi vu d'en haut, le paysage tout entier avait l'air immobile comme une peinture; les navires à l'ancre se tassaient dans un coin; le fleuve arrondissait sa courbe au pied des collines vertes, et les îles, de forme oblongue, semblaient sur l'eau de grands poissons noirs arrêtés. Les cheminées des usines poussaient d'immenses panaches bruns qui s'envolaient par le bout. On entendait le ronflement des fonderies avec le carillon clair des églises qui se dressaient dans la brume. Les arbres des boulevards, sans feuilles, faisaient des broussailles violettes au milieu des maisons, et les toits, tout reluisants de pluie, miroitaient inégalement, selon la hauteur des quartiers. Parfois un coup de vent emportait les nuages vers la côte Saint-Catherine, comme des flots aériens qui se brisaient en silence contre une falaise. (393–4)[35]

Sloping downward like an amphitheatre, drowned in mist, it sprawled out shapelessly beyond its bridges. Then open fields swept upward again in a monotonous curve, merging at the top with the uncertain line of the pale sky. Thus seen from above, the whole landscape had the static quality of a painting; ships at anchor were crowded into one corner, the river traced its curve along the foot of the green hills, and on the water the oblong-shaped islands looked like great black fish stopped in their course. From the factory chimneys poured endless trails of brown smoke, their tips continually dissolving in the wind. The roar of foundries mingled with the clear peal of chimes that came from the churches looming in the fog. The leafless trees along the boulevards were like purple thickets in amongst the houses; and the roofs, all of them shiny with rain, gleamed with particular brilliance in the upper reaches of the town. Now and again a gust of wind blew the clouds toward the hill of Sainte-Catherine, like aerial waves breaking soundlessly against a cliff. (299)

(12) Shortly afterward comes the first appearance of the appalling blind man, referred to only as *l'aveugle*:

Il y avait dans la côte un pauvre diable vagabondant avec son bâton, tout au milieu des diligences. Un amas de guenilles lui recouvrait les épaules, et un vieux castor défoncé, s'arrondissant en cuvette, lui cachait la figure; mais, quand il le retirait, il découvrait, à la place des paupières, deux orbites béantes tout ensanglantées. La chair s'effilo-quait par lambeaux rouges; et il en coulait des liquides qui se figeaient en gales vertes jusqu'au nez, dont les narines noires reniflaient con-vulsivement. Pour vous parler, il se renversait la tête avec un rire idiot; – alors ses prunelles bleuâtres, roulant d'un mouvement continu, allaient se cogner, vers les tempes, sur le bord de la plaie vive. (399)

On this hill-road was a wretched beggar, who wandered with his stick in the midst of the traffic. His clothes were a mass of rags, and his face was hidden under a battered old felt hat that was turned down all around like a basin; when he took this off, it was to reveal two gaping, bloody sockets in place of eyelids. The flesh continually shred-ded off in red gobbets, and from it oozed a liquid matter, hardening into greenish scabs that reached down to his nose. His black nostrils sniffed convulsively. Whenever he began to talk, he leaned his head far back and gave an idiot laugh; and at such times his bluish eyeballs, rolling round and round, pushed up against the edges of the live wound. (303–4)

(13) A page later, still on the *aveugle*:

Souvent, on était en marche, lorsque son chapeau, d'un mouvement brusque entrait dans la diligence par le vasistas, tandis qu'il se cram-ponnait, de l'autre bras, sur le marchepied, entre l'éclaboussure des roues. Sa voix, faible d'abord et vagissante, devenait aiguë. Elle se traînait dans la nuit, comme l'indistincte lamentation d'une vague détresse; et, à travers la sonnerie des grelots, le murmure des arbres et le ronflement de la boîte creuse, elle avait quelque chose de lointain qui bouleversait Emma. (400)

Often while the coach was moving slowly up the hill his hat would suddenly come through the window, and he would be there, clinging with his other hand to the footboard, between the spattering wheels. His voice, at the outset a mere wail, would grow shrill. It would linger in the darkness like a plaintive cry of distress; and through the jingle of the horse bells, the rustle of the trees and the rumble of the empty coach, there was something eerie about it that gave Emma a shudder of horror. (304)

(14) Inevitably, the voice of the blind man returns to trouble Emma's deathbed:

Tout à coup, on entendit sur le trottoir un bruit de gros sabots, avec le frôlement d'un bâton; et une voix s'éleva, une voix rauque, qui chantait:

Souvent la chaleur d'un beau jour
Fait rêver fillette à l'amour.

Emma se releva comme un cadavre que l'on galvanise, les cheveux dénoués, la prunelle fixe, béante.

Pour amasser diligemment
Les épis que la faux moissonne,
Ma Nanette va s'inclinant
Vers le sillon qui nous les donne.

– L'aveugle! s'écria-t-elle.

Et Emma se mit à rire, d'un rire atroce, frénétique, désespéré, croyant voir la face hideuse du misérable, qui se dressait dans les ténèbres éternelles comme un épouvantement.

Il souffla bien fort ce jour-là.
Et le jupon court s'envola!

Une convulsion la rabattit sur le matelas. Tous s'approchèrent. Elle n'existait plus. (472)

Suddenly from out on the sidewalk came a noise of heavy wooden shoes and the scraping of a stick, and a voice rose up, a raucous voice singing:

A clear day's warm will often move
A lass to stray in dreams of love.

Emma sat up like a galvanized corpse, her hair streaming, her eyes fixed and gaping.

To gather up the stalks of wheat

> *The swinging scythe keeps laying by,*
> *Nanette goes stooping in the heat*
> *Along the furrows where they lie.*

"The blind man!" she cried.

Emma began to laugh – a horrible, frantic, desperate laugh – fancying that she saw the beggar's hideous face, a figure of terror looming up in the darkness of eternity.

> *The wind blew very hard that day*
> *And snatched her petticoat away!*

A spasm had flung her down on the mattress. Everyone drew close. She had ceased to exist. (369–70)

(15) A final quotation comes from the last pages of the novel, when Charles and Rodolphe meet by chance at a market and sit down together in a cabaret:

L'autre [Rodolphe] continuait à parler culture, bestiaux, engrais, bouchant avec des phrases banales tous les interstices où pouvait se glisser une allusion. Charles ne l'écoutait pas; Rodolphe s'en apercevait, et il suivait sur la mobilité de sa figure le passage des souvenirs. Elle s'empourprait peu à peu, les narines battaient vite, les lèvres frémissaient; il y eut même un instant où Charles, plein d'une fureur sombre, fixa ses yeux contre Rodolphe qui, dans une sorte d'effroi, s'interrompit. Mais bientôt la même lassitude funèbre réapparut sur son visage. (500)

Rodolphe talked farming, livestock, fertilizers – making use of banalities to stop up all the gaps through which any compromising reference might creep in. Charles wasn't listening. Rodolphe became aware of this; and in the play of expression on Charles's face he could read the sequence of his thoughts. Gradually it grew crimson; Charles's nostrils fluttered, his lips quivered; at one point, filled with somber fury, he stared fixedly at Rodolphe, who in his fright had stopped speaking. But almost at once the other man's features resumed their habitual expression of mournful weariness. (395)

4

Looking over the above citations (and the others in this essay), several points emerge:

(1) As the page references suggest, alliterative and assonance- or consonance-filled passages such as these do not make up a continuous fabric in the novel. There are many more of them than I have indicated, but they are intermittent; pages go by without such a passage striking one (which is not to say that those pages are devoid of such activity). In addition, not all the passages I have cited are equally dense or "active" in this regard. The last citation in particular is less striking in its own right than in relation to the ones that have gone before. But that by no means invalidates its interest for us in this connection.

(2) Sometimes, as in the fourth of the citations, describing Emma warming herself at the fire in the inn kitchen as Léon looks on, the phonemic activity – keyed in this instance to *ch*, hard *c*, *p*, *t*, and *v* (at the very least) – is in effect masked or say dimmed by the extraordinary vividness of the tableau as a whole, even as, I want to claim, that activity contributes to the vividness in some difficult to specify manner for the alert or sensitized or otherwise prepared reader. Something similar takes place in the fifth passage, Lheureux exhibiting his wares, in the eleventh, the evocation of the countryside en route to Rouen and then Rouen itself (note, among other repetitions, the sequence "arrondissait," "oblongue," "poissons," "on," "ronflement," "fonderies," "carillon," "maisons"), and in the initial description of the blind man as well as in the next to last of the passages, in which the extraordinary salience of the consonant *v* – four in the short sentence beginning "Emma se releva . . ." – can easily go unnoticed amid the (admittedly somewhat contrived) horror of what is taking place.

(3) Certain letters or sounds tend to predominate in the passages in question, in particular *p*, *t*, hard *c*, and, to a remarkable degree, *v*. Here I can only ask my reader to look those passages over again, and even perhaps to keep count as he or she does so. So for example the second ("Elle étudia, dans Eugène Sue, . . .") contains twenty-four *v*'s; the third ("Au fond de son âme, cependant, . . ."), eleven; the fourth ("Madame Bovary, quand elle fut dans la cuisine, . . ."), only six, but they become

more frequent toward the end of the paragraph, culminating in Léon's "chevelure blonde"; the fifth and sixth ("Alors M. Lheureux exhiba . . ." and "Cependant les flammes s'apaisèrent . . .") largely forgo *v* in favor of *p*, another favorite letter/sound, as in the "Cependant, sous la pluie des pensums" citation with which this essay began, though it should be said the fifth also is especially rich in repetitions of all sorts; the seventh ("Il arriva dans son cabriolet . . .") is a tissue of *v*'s, hard *c*'s, and *p*'s; the eighth ("La diligence descendait . . .") contains no fewer than twenty-three *v*'s along with repeated *p*'s and hard *c*'s; the ninth ("De peur de paraître ridicule, . . .") has more *p*'s than *v*'s but together they dominate the sound-pattern of the two paragraphs to an impressive degree (twenty-one *p*'s, nine *v*'s, culminating in the surprising noun "désinvolture"); the first cita-tion of the tenth example (". . . Il devait avoir, pensait-elle . . .") contains twelve *v*'s, and the tenth ("L'odeur du gaz . . ."), still at the opera, eight, with four coming in the final sentence; the twelfth ("Il y avait dans la côté un pauvre diable . . .") deploys sixteen *v*'s and ten hard *c*'s; the thirteenth ("Souvent, on était un marche, . . .") has ten *v*'s; and the fourteenth, Emma's last moments, contains seventeen, five of which turn up in the blind man's song. (Here I cannot resist quoting again the astonishing sen-tence, "Emma se releva comme un cadavre que l'on galvanise, les cheveux dénoués, la prunelle fixe, béante." Note too the *m*'s and *n*'s.)[36] The last quotation, the non-conversation between Charles and Rodolphe, includes eight *v*-words, including the last, "visage," but equally present are *p*'s, *b*'s, and *f*s. As for example eleven ("Descendant tout en amphithéâtre . . ."), it has eleven *v*-words, but what is truly spectacular, from the present point of view, is the unrelieved density of phonemic play generally. Indeed the paragraph that follows (394–5) is comparably dense and contains thirteen *v*-words – in fact these few pages mark a virtual irruption of such play. (Look back, too, to the paragraph cited earlier describing the invitees to Charles and Emma's wedding, beginning, "Les conviés arrivèrent de bonne heure dans des voitures, carrioles à un cheval," with its fourteen *v*-words in three sentences.)

Once more, then: how are we to understand what is going on? Obvi-ously it is to the point, how could it not be, that the letter *v* (to stay with that for the moment) occurs prominently in the name "Bovary"; that it is crucial to what Culler has called Flaubert's "vealism," the novel's obsessional play with the word "veau" and its variants and homonyms as in "nouveau," "Vaubyessard,"[37] "Vaufrylard" (a name used by Flaubert himself, it will be remembered – the adjective "bovin" also is to the point), and "Tuvache" (mayor of Yonville-l'Abbaye, "vache" of course being the French for "cow"); that the letter *v* begins the word "vacarme" and occurs in "charivari" (as it does in "Charbovari"), to which we must add that it also appears in the names of the two doctors "Canivet" and "Larivière" as well as in that of "Hivert," the coachman of *l'Hirondelle* (notice, by the way, how *l'Hirondelle* carries "elle" within it), and that it begins the title (the not-quite-name) "Vicomte" as well as the sinister name "Vinçart," a character who never makes an appearance but whom the dreadful Lheureux claims is demanding payment from Emma. Plus there is "Yonville" itself and in Rouen "la place Beauvoisine" (where there is an inn full of "vacarme"). At a crucial moment in their developing relations, Charles and Emma are briefly brought together by a dropped "cravache" (or whip), also called a "nerf de boeuf," thus further activating the "veau"-complex. (Later she gives Rodolphe a present of a "cravache à pommeau de vermeil" [a riding crop with a silver-gilt knob]. Rodolphe's mistress at the time he meets Emma, by the way, is one "Virginie.") Following the ball at Vaubyessard, Emma prizes "le porte-cigares en soie verte" [the cigar-case trimmed with green silk] that she likes to think belonged to the Vicomte; she breathes in the odor of its lining, "mêlée de verveine et de tabac" [fragrant with verbena and tobacco]; when she dreams about Paris it shines for her "dans une atmosphere vermeille" (in a rosy atmosphere). After Emma's death, Homais's thought is to build in her honor a temple to "Vesta," but that may be pushing things, as may the fact that the young Emma made a drawing of a head of "Minerve." We are also told that the real-life author of the book on the treatment of clubfoot which Charles studies before attempting to cure Hippolyte is named Duval, that Charles at the moment of the amputation of Hippolyte's leg exclaims, "Mais c'était peut-être un valgus!" ["I wonder – could it perhaps have been a valgus?"], and that Emma as a young girl was deeply moved by Bernardin de Saint-Pierre's *Paul et Virginie* (lending the name of Rodolphe's mistress

a further tinge of irony). All this together with the fact, established by Edi
Zollinger, of Flaubert's preoccupation throughout *Madame Bovary* – if
Zollinger is right, starting with the title – with Victor Hugo, the still vital
literary titan of an earlier generation, and in particular with his prose masterpiece *Notre-Dame de Paris*. (Throughout the years 1851–6 Flaubert was
in touch with Hugo, who of course was in self-willed exile on Guernsey,
and in fact played an active role in receiving and forwarding letters on the
great man's behalf.)[38]

But what precisely is the point that we are to take away from these
observations? On the one hand, there can be no doubt as to the strength
of Flaubert's investment in two independent but potentially mutually
reinforcing networks, the first keyed to the word "veau" and its various
cognates, the second based on a multifaceted relationship to an earlier
novel by a great writer whose first name begins precisely with the letter
v – a letter, it is worth remarking, that occurs relatively infrequently in
standard French.[39] On the other hand, are we to conclude from this, is it
even remotely conceivable, that each occurrence of the letter *v* in the passages quoted above – again, how best to put this? – was actively intended
by the author to "belong" to one or the other of those networks, or
indeed to both at the same time, to a greater or lesser degree? That seems
impossible. For that matter, is it quite imaginable that each of those recurrences was recognized as such, as a separate and distinct instance of the
consonant *v*, by Flaubert at some moment or other in the production of
the final text? For all his talk of the "gueuloir" and of his "chasse aux assonances," that too seems extremely unlikely. Can we even be certain that
in a sentence like "Emma se releva comme un cadavre que l'on galvanise,
les cheveux dénoués, la prunelle fixe, béante," he would have registered
the interplay of *v*'s (not to mention the six *n*'s) separately from the words
in which they appear? And if not there, where the four *v*'s almost jostle
one another, how can we imagine that he would have done so anywhere
else? And yet, to come full circle, does it follow, can we possibly be sure,
that every not obviously "veau"-based or Victor Hugo-allusive recurrence
of the letter *v* has absolutely nothing to do – is in no sense in communi-
cation – with those two conceptual frameworks?

The question, in other words, is one of authorial intention, or rather of authorial intention insofar as the notion may be held to imply a certain minimum degree, even the merest trace, of authorial self-awareness, specifically – in this case – with respect to recurrences of the letter *v*. And what gives this question its particular edge, of course, is the new and special role that the notion of authorial intention or say will, "volonté," has always been understood to play in Flaubert's literary enterprise, in the first instance in the writing of *Madame Bovary*, along with a new ideal of authorial impersonality. (The second essay in this book will be concerned with the role of "volonté" in the writing and reading of *Salammbô*.) The classic *profession de foi* by Flaubert himself comes from a letter to an admiring reader, Mlle Leroyer de Chantepie, whose intense sympathy for Emma led her to find in the novel equivalents of her own life experiences. "*Madame Bovary* has nothing 'true' in it," Flaubert replied to her in a letter of 18 March 1857. "It is a *totally invented* story; into it I put none of my own feelings and nothing from my own life. The illusion (if there is one) comes, on the contrary, from the *impersonality* of the work. It is a principle of mine that one must not *write oneself* [*s'écrire*]. The artist must be like God in his creation, invisible and all-powerful: he must be everywhere felt, but never seen."[40] *Qu'on le sente partout* – throughout the full extent of his creation but also, so to speak, down to the smallest units of it as well – as regards *Madame Bovary*, in every word, syllable, phoneme, vowel, consonant, indeed in every punctuation mark, every "coupe" (Albert Thibaudet's term, referring to Flaubert's mastery of commas, full stops, "arrêts de tous genres").[41] And *tout-puissant* – without limitation of any sort on what he may be understood to have brought about. In his nephew and disciple Guy de Maupassant's succinct, brilliant formulation: "Gustave Flaubert, in fact, was the most ardent apostle of impersonality in art. He would not admit that the author ever should be surmised, that he should let fall in a page, in a line, in a word, a single particle of his opinion, nothing but an appearance of intention [*rien qu'une apparence d'intention*]" (viii; translation modified).[42] What Maupassant implies but does not quite say is that the revolutionary impersonality of Flaubert's prose ("L'apparition de *Madame Bovary* fut une Révolution dans les lettres," he writes a page or so earlier [563]) not only coexists with but in effect continually throws into relief the "apparence d'intention," which thereby presides both extensively and intensively – sweepingly and minutely – over the text from first sentence to last.

This of course was not Ricardou's perspective on the issue that intrigued him. As we saw, Ricardou claimed to have found in *Madame Bovary* several striking instances of a more general phenomenon, the primacy in literary texts of a conflict between both narrative and description on the one hand and the autonomous-seeming play of language, of linguistic signifiers, on the other. (His key examples involved the recurrence of the letters *c* and *b* in the description of Charles's "casquette"; the discovery, as it seemed to him, of the name-form BOVRI in the same passage; the association of "Charbovari" with "charivari" and thence to "vacarme"; and the importance of "veau"-words for the novel as a whole.) None of this, in his view, could be accounted for by an appeal to authorial intention; rather, what was at stake was a level of signifying activity that belonged in effect to language alone, or literary language alone. Granted, Roussel, whom he greatly admired, had consciously constructed similar effects, which nevertheless had gone unrecognized until Roussel himself pointed them out. But Ricardou insisted that the question of conscious intention was secondary, and that what mattered, in his view, was the nature of the effects, not so to speak their cause. (Or as he also put it, the process but not the means by which the process came about.) Such a stance toward his observations understandably failed to satisfy his interlocutors, who pointed out that the entire "veau"-network of names and words could only have been deliberately plotted by Flaubert, as is plainly the case. More broadly, Françoise Gaillard insisted that to the extent that the linguistic activity Ricardou had called attention to merited further discussion (at a minimum, let us say, the prevalence of *c*- and *b*-words in the description of the "casquette"), the question could legitimately be raised as to how that activity was to be explained. As she put it, he owed an account of the "theory of the subject" implied by his observations, the further gist of her remarks being that she understood this to require acknowledging the operations of something like the Freudian unconscious.

In *Nouveaux problèmes du roman*, where he returned to the topic, Ricardou attempted to meet Gaillard halfway by adapting a Freudian framework to his own not quite Freudian purposes. So for example he argued that "there is a consonance that is *wild* and unconscious in that it takes place, if one can say that, for itself, outside the unconscious intention of the operator," associating that "consonance" with the tendency of young children at the stage of acquiring language to find pleasure in playing with words "'without concern for the meaning of words or the coherence of sentences' [a quotation from Freud]."[43] Immediately, however, that tendency is placed under censure by the superego, which Ricardou understands as serving a larger cultural and ideological injunction that in effect subordinates the materiality of language to the primacy of meaning. Literature, on his account, is precisely where the effects of that censure can be best escaped – hence "the abundance of wild unconscious consonances in literature, understood here as the set of texts that come out of a very special language effort" (81). Finally, Ricardou posits two contradictory "tendencies" (the French is "versants") in the unconscious: one rhetorical, the other poetic, the first essentially regressive, the second aggressive, the first associated with psychoanalysis and the second with poetry. "In short," he concludes, "alongside the healing effects of psychoanalysis, we would have to admit the specific effects, let us say easing effects at the least, of the exercise of literature" (83). Such as, presumably, the play of consonants and other letters to be observed in the passages from *Madame Bovary* cited above.

5

Where has all this brought us? Here is where it has *not* brought us: to a juncture at which I shall seek to determine, for each of the passages in question, and specifically for the particular instances of consonantal or phonemic play that they comprise, to what extent we are dealing with products of authorial intention as distinct from the results of some sort of unconscious, in that sense automatistic, linguistic process, whether we choose to think of that process in Ricardou's quasi-psychoanalytic terms or not. Put slightly differently, there can be no question but that certain linguistic and proto-linguistic phenomena that we have considered – all those associated with Flaubert's "vealism," for a start, as well as others discovered by Zollinger in *Arachnes Rache* – were consciously intended as such by the author. What, however, of the others? I have already said that I regard it as extremely unlikely (to put it mildly) that Flaubert can be imagined acknowledging each of them in turn, again as such, as one by one they passed through the loud and demanding test of the "gueuloir." But it does not follow that none of or for that matter no cluster of those assonances, consonances, and repetitions was consciously acknowledged by him at one or another stage of the writing process; that too seems highly improbable. Or take what I have described as the irruption of dense phonemic play in the pages associated with example eleven: now it is an interesting fact that this occurs at a crucial juncture in the narrative – Emma's embarking recklessly on her affair with Léon. But is it at all likely that Flaubert intended to mark that juncture in this way? I suspect not. And yet is it wholly beside the point that the pages in question are found precisely there? That too seems far from certain. So we are left with the thought of a supreme literary masterwork, often viewed as *the* revolutionary achievement in the history of the modern novel, which turns out to be marked by two seemingly antithetical characteristics: on the one hand, a new and altogether radical thematization of writerly intention, directed toward the actualization of an almost unattainable ideal of stylistic perfection and imagined as essentially divorced from the expression of any merely contingent feature of the writer's life and opinions; and second, the proliferation throughout the novel of an extraordinary range and variety of linguistic and proto-linguistic effects categorizable, more or less, with the aid of terms like assonance, consonance, alliteration, rhymes, off-rhymes, resemblances between words and names, repetitions and near-repetitions of all sorts, and so on, some significant portion of which is attributable, it would seem, to something other than authorial control. And I suggest, too, that this doubleness, the manifest coexistence of just these antithetical or seemingly antithetical characteristics, is *the* defining feature of *Madame Bovary* as a work of artistic prose. If the present essay is found to make a persuasive case for this view of Flaubert's first great novel, I will regard it as having achieved its aim. (Let it remain an open question whether anything exactly or even approximately comparable to this state of affairs can be found elsewhere in modern literature.)

But I do not quite want to stop here. To say that *Madame Bovary* exhibits these antithetical characteristics is also to say that each is deeply, even inextricably implicated in the other. Thus the simultaneously overarching and fine-grained thematization of authorial intention means that there is no verbal or phonemic or otherwise proto-linguistic incident, however slight, that can wholly escape the gravitational field of Flaubert's writerly project (we can never be certain that a given instance of phonemic play is an "accidental" event and nothing more), just as there are no instances of manifest intention that can wholly escape the implication of a certain automaticity in the mode of their production (thus the "veau"-network cannot be cordoned off from the prevalence of the consonant *v* in passage after passage that has nothing to do with cow imagery in any respect).

To take two more brief examples we have not yet glanced at, here is a short paragraph evoking a stage in Emma's recovery from the collapse of her hopes following Rodolphe's sudden departure:

> Vers le milieu d'octobre, elle put se tenir assise dans son lit, avec des oreillers derrière elle. Charles pleura quand il la vit manger sa première tartine de confitures. Les forces lui revinrent; elle se levait quelques heures pendant l'après-midi, et, un jour qu'elle se sentait mieux, il essaya de lui faire faire, à son bras, un tour de promenade dans le jardin. Le sable des allées disparaissait sous les feuilles mortes; elle marchait pas à pas, en trainant ses pantoufles, et, s'appuyant de l'épaule contre Charles, elle continuait à sourire. (324–5)

Toward the middle of October she could sit up in bed, propped against pillows. Charles wept when he saw her eat her first slice of bread and jam. Her strength returned; she left her bed for a few hours each afternoon; and one day when she felt better than usual he got her to take his arm and try a walk in the garden. The gravel on the paths was almost hidden under dead leaves; she walked slowly, dragging her slippers; and leaning on Charles's shoulder she smiled continuously. (236)

On the one hand, the paragraph seems a perfectly modulated specimen of Flaubert's prose, just four sentences long, the first two simple, the second two more complex, wholly focused on the narrative / descriptive task at hand. In that sense, the repetitions of the letters *p*, *t*, *s*, early on *v*, later on *f*, also *m*'s and *n*'s, can be understood in purely local terms, as helping to articulate and body forth a specific *tableau mouvant*. On the other, the prevalence of the letter *p* throughout the passage leads one to recall the frequency with which it appears throughout the novel, starting with the "Cependant, sous la pluie des pensums, . . ." paragraph in chapter one, which is to say that the implication of a certain automaticity, of the merely habitual (to introduce a term that will become more important shortly), cannot be gainsaid. This comes to a head in the last sentence with the sequence "dis*p*araissait," "*p*as à *p*as," "*p*antoufles," "s'ap*p*uyant" and "l'é*p*aule," which seems excessive, does it not? – once one notices it, that is. As does, dispersed across the last two sentences, the less obvious sequence "*f*orces," "*f*aire *f*aire," "*f*euilles," and "pantou*f*les." (On the next rereading the excessiveness can dissipate. On the one following it can return.) There is even a sense, rereading the paragraph in the light of my arguments so far – also in the light of observations by commentators such as Starobinksi, Duchet, and Ricardou – in which the unit *p*/*t* can almost seem to play a generating role vis-à-vis the sentences in which it appears, coming into focus in the phrase "tour de promenade" and culminating in the word "pantoufles," in which so much of the phonemic play of the previous lines comes to a head. (For Duchet, presumably, this would be explained by the primacy of objects in Flaubert's literary *imaginaire*, whether or not the writer consciously intended the phonemic play to that end. No doubt he would have the same view of the paragraph, also including "pantoufles," in which Lheureux begins his temptation of Emma.)

As for the second example, I am aware that this is likely to seem the rankest overkill, but here as further evidence of a certain stake in the unit

p/t (or perhaps $p/t/s$ or even $p/t/s/b$) is a short, justly admired paragraph from the *baisade*, the initial seduction of Emma by Rodolphe following their ride in the woods. The paragraph belongs to the preliminaries:

> A côté, sur la pelouse, entre les sapins, une lumière brune circulait dans l'atmosphère tiède. La terre, roussâtre comme de la poudre de tabac, amortissait le bruit des pas; et, du bout de leurs fers, en marchant, les chevaux poussaient devant eux des pommes de pin tombées. (261)

> To one side, over the turf between the firs, the light was dim and the air mild. The reddish earth, the color of snuff, deadened the sound of the hoofs; and the horses kicked fir cones before them as they walked. (178–9)

Considered in isolation, this too is an instance of Flaubert's prose at its most exquisitely descriptive. Once again, though, it belongs to a larger structure of repetitions that runs through the novel as a whole.

Let me be clear: I am not suggesting that in the last analysis the auto-matistic, habitual perspective is the correct or the dominant one – the "isolated" view of passages such as the last two we have glanced at cannot simply be brushed aside or subordinated to the play of alliteration, asso-nance, and phonemic relationships generally. My point is rather that throughout *Madame Bovary* the intentional and the automatistic and habit-ual not only actively coexist but so to speak interpenetrate one another, to the extent that they everywhere compete for salience, at any rate in the act of reading as exemplified by the present essay.[44]

Some such experience of the text perhaps lies behind Charles Du Bos's surprising characterization in "Sur le milieu intérieur chez Flaubert" of a particular "disproportion" that he finds in Flaubert's prose and which he claims has not escaped any attentive reader:

> It could not be said that individual words are, in themselves, too over-powering; the expression is almost always perfectly right, singularly strong in its aptness. The disproportion does not reside in the expres-sion itself, but in all the restrictions that have had to be satisfied in order

to reach it. Once "put in place" every word undoubtedly reveals its full "power": it always seems vigorous and dense, sometimes splendid, sometimes with a slightly opaque brilliance. But it always seems to overflow into the neighboring space, if only by the robustness with which it occupies the place so dearly conquered, with the result that between the words there do not circulate those breaths of divine inspiration ["la *mens divinior*"] that guarantee the interlinking of the whole ["la liaison"]. Let me not be misunderstood: the continuity of Flaubert's style is indeed, to quote Marcel Proust's perfect expression, "hermetic"; but it is so much so that the blanks that separate the words are only blanks in effect: between [or across] them there is no play; there is a lack of that linkage [or *legato*], the glory of the supreme instrumentalists, of that most ineffable of qualities which is like the air in which the style bathes. I know of no other great writer in whose style there is as little air as in Flaubert's; he must be very great indeed for us not to regret it more often than we do. That we can even come to cherish this lack of proportion is the best measure of his importance and validity. (365; extensively modified)[45]

(In a footnote, Du Bos adds, "There are no holes [*trous*] in Flaubert's style; to the least fissure, he always prefers a heaviness, even an awkwardness.") The "disproportion," in short, concerns the mode of interaction between the words or expressions and their respective settings – in terms of the present essay, a hypertrophy of phonemic relations (repetitions, anticipations, close variations) that at once firmly secures the placement of the individual word or phrase and continually calls into question the very distinction between word or phrase and setting. The proliferation of such relations, running through entire paragraphs, and beyond that throughout the novel as a whole, conduces to what Du Bos describes as an absence of "air," the filling of "trous" and "fissures" of all sorts; it is also what leads him to say that the blank spaces between words are blanks only "in effect" – nominally, not efficaciously. At the same time, his closing sentences acknowledge – with a hint of puzzlement – that this very "disproportion" is somehow central to Flaubert's remarkable achievement.

In a similar spirit, Proust, in the essay referred to by Du Bos, introduces the contemporary image of a moving sidewalk to characterize the effect of Flaubert's prose. "And no one who has once climbed on to the great *Moving pavement* [*Trottoir roulant*] that are the pages of Flaubert, as they file continuously, monotonously, indefinitely past, can possibly fail to recognize that they are without precedent in literature" (262; emphasis in original).[46] Proust also emphasizes, as noted earlier and as recalled by Du Bos, the "hermetic continuity of [Flaubert's] style," indeed in advance of Du Bos he notes how Flaubert fills up "the smallest holes," along with offering superb analyses of two key features of Flaubert's prose – his use of the imperfect followed by the present participle and of the conjunction "et" – that contribute to that effect. Above all, though, Proust singles out for special notice a certain heaviness-cum-mechanicalness in Flaubert's style. As he puts it:

> Yet we love those heavy materials which Flaubert's sentences lift and let fall again with the intermittent noise of an excavator. For if, as has been written, Flaubert's lamp at night served seafarers as a lighthouse, one might also say that the sentences emitted through his "gueuloir" had the regular rhythm of the machines that are used for clearing away spoil. Fortunate those who are alive to this obsessive rhythm . . . (268)[47]

The spoil or "déblais," I am suggesting, may be associated with the fragments of words – vowels, consonants, phonemes, syllables, repetitions of all kinds – that it has been the purpose of this essay to bring to the fore. And the unexpected turn of Proust's characteristically inventive metaphor is that it was precisely the operation of the "gueuloir," whose ostensible purpose was to expunge such repetitive micro-entities from his writing, that produced those fragments whose rhythmic "falling" he found so strangely attractive.*

---

* Cf. Roland Barthes's penetrating summary of the first of two "crosses" Flaubert had to bear when he corrected his manuscripts. "The first cross," Barthes writes, "is the repetition of words; it is a matter of substitutive correction here, since it is the (phonic) form

6

At this point I want to make a rather abrupt transition with the help of still another episode from the novel. Charles's misconceived attempt to cure Hippolyte's clubfoot has come definitively to grief. Canivet, the distinguished doctor who will amputate the leg, has just arrived at the *Lion d'or* "comme un tourbillon," but in his usual manner has made sure that his horse was properly stabled and was feeding on oats before turning to the task at hand. "On disait même à ce propos: 'Ah! M. Canivet, c'est un original!'" the text informs us. "Et on l'estimait davantage pour cet inébranlable aplomb. L'univers aurait pu crever jusqu'au dernier homme, qu'il n'eût pas failli à la moindre de ses habitudes." (290) ["'That Canivet – he's a character!' people said of him; and they thought the more of him for his unshakable self-assurance. The universe might have perished to the last man, and he wouldn't have altered his habits a jot." (206)]

Homais then presents himself to the famous doctor, who immediately asks him to assist in the operation; true to type, Homais declines, explain-

---

of the word whose too-immediate return must be avoided, while retaining the content; as we have said, the possibilities of correction are limited here, which should lighten the writer's responsibility all the more; yet here Flaubert manages to introduce the vertigo of an infinite correction: the difficulty, for him, is not correction itself (actually limited), but discernment of the place where it is necessary: certain repetitions appear, which had not been noticed the day before, so that nothing can guarantee that the next day new 'mistakes' will not be discovered; thus, there develops an anxious insecurity, for it always seems possible to *hear* new repetitions: the text, even when it has been meticulously worked over, is somehow *mined* with risks of repetition: limited and consequently reassured in its act, substitution again becomes free and consequently agonizing by the infinity of its possible emplacements: the paradigm is of course closed, but since it functions with each significative unit, it is seized again by the infinity of the syntagm" ("Flaubert and the Sentence," in *New Critical Essays*, trans. Richard Howard [New York, 1980], 74; emphasis in original). On the next page Barthes cites in a note a remark from one of Flaubert's letters to Louise Colet: "I ended by leaving off the corrections; I had reached the point where I understood nothing – pressing too hard on a piece of work, it dazzles you; what seems to be wrong now in five minutes seems perfectly all right; it's a series of corrections and recorrections that never comes to an end" (75–6; *Corr.*, 2: 372–3, 2 July 1853). (The last clause is not cited by Barthes but is obviously to the point.)

ing that he has so nervous a system – at which point Canivet cuts him off and contrasts him with himself:

> "Regardez-moi, plutôt: tous les jours, je me lève à quatre heures, je fais ma barbe à l'eau froide (je n'ai jamais froid), et je ne porte pas de flanelle, je n'attrape aucun rhume, le coffre est bon! Je vis tantôt d'une manière, tantôt d'une autre, en philosophe, au hasard de la fourchette. C'est pourquoi je ne suis point délicat comme vous, et il m'est aussi parfaitement égal de découper un Chrétien que la première volaille venue. Après ça, direz-vous, l'habitude . . . , l'habitude! . . ." (291)

> "Look at me: I'm up every day at four, shave in cold water every season of the year; I'm never chilly, never wear flannel underwear, never catch cold – I'm sound as a bell. I eat well one day, badly the next, however it comes. I take it philosophically. That's why I'm not a bit squeamish, like you. And that's why it's all the same to me whether I carve up a Christian or any old chicken they put in front of me. Beyond that, you will say, it's habit . . . habit . . ." (206)[48]

My point in citing the above is not primarily to emphasize its pattern of alliterations (five *f*'s in the first sentence of Canivet's self-description, with the unexpected word "fourchette" bringing the second to a close; for that matter, four *v*'s in the previous citation), but rather to call attention to the somewhat surprising portrayal of the supremely competent doctor as a man of habit.

More precisely, my thought is that the thematizing of the idea of habit at this juncture may have some broader significance for the novel as a whole. For example, it seems possible to understand Canivet's mode of life (his "inébranlable aplomb") as epitomizing a deliberate denial of personal moods and feelings, or say a kind of determined impersonality ("I have no personal feelings, it is all one to me whether I am cutting up a chicken or a human being"). This would constitute a link of sorts with Flaubert's authorial ideal, and in fact Canivet has been regarded by more than one commentator as a stand-in for Flaubert. (In the next paragraph we are told that Canivet regards his "art" as a "sacerdoce," which could not be more Flaubertian. Flaubert's father, Achille-Cléophas, was the chief surgeon and director of the Hôtel-Dieu in Rouen.) But it would also be to associate that ideal with (mere) habit, which is to say (it would seem) with mechanical repetition – for example, of vowels, consonants, phonemes, etc. – rather than with artistic intentions as they are usually understood. Note, however, that the initial identification of Canivet as a man of habit is in free indirect style, that is, it expresses the general view of his actions, and that Canivet in his exchange with Homais uses the formulation "direz-vous" ("you will say"), meaning that he knows that his life is seen and described by others in that light, leaving open the question of his own view of it. In terms of the analogy between Canivet and Flaubert, this would be to acknowledge that *one possible account* of the latter's enterprise in *Madame Bovary* would stress the role of habit as mere mechanical repetition and at the same time implicitly to disavow such an acount in favor of a different but unstated understanding of the matter (such an understanding, in Canivet's case, would be bound to emphasize his determination, his confirmed intention, to pursue a certain form of life).

The risk in all this, of course, is that it comes close to finding in the paragraphs in question a key to Flaubert's project as a whole, an interpretive move I don't quite wish to make even as their thematization of the concept of habit seems to me to warrant as much attention as one is prepared to give it. In this connection I want to introduce a text that lies outside the Flaubertian corpus and indeed has never to my knowledge been linked in any way with his writing – the philosopher Félix Ravaisson's short treatise *De l'habitude* (1838).[49] I realize, how could I not, that this is bound to come as something of a shock in view of the hermeticism, to adapt Proust's term, of my critical procedures so far in this essay. But I hope the reason for such a step will become clear soon enough.

Briefly, then, Jean-Gaspard-Félix Ravaisson was born in 1813 in comfortable circumstances. An exceptional student, he attended the Collège Rollin in Paris, where he won top prizes. In 1834 he won a competition held by the Académie des Sciences morales et politiques with a study of Aristotle's *Metaphysics*, later revised and published in two volumes as *Essai sur la métaphysique d'Aristote.* Shortly afterward he is thought to have attended Friedrich Schelling's philosophy lectures in Munich, perhaps on the recommendation of Victor Cousin, then a major force in French academic philosophy. In 1837 he came out on top of the *agrégation* in philosophy, and submitted *De l'habitude* – not a tome but rather a treatise of roughly 14,000 words – to the Sorbonne as his doctoral thesis. It was published in 1838. An academic career was open to him, but instead he chose to enter the civil service, serving first as Inspector of Libraries and eventually as Inspector General of Higher Education; this enabled him to live in Paris and move in the fashionable society that suited him. In 1867 he published an ambitious work commissioned by the government, *Rapport sur la philosophie en France au XIXème siècle*, which exerted a strong influence over philosophical education in France for several decades. Ravaisson was also deeply involved in the arts; he drew more than competently, studied painting with Jacques-Louis David's student Jean Broc, and went on to exhibit portraits at the Salon. In 1870 he was appointed curator of classical antiquities at the Louvre, where he was in charge of the restoration of the *Venus de Milo*. (Earlier he had been responsible for a report on the teaching of drawing in schools.) This by no means covers all his publications. In short he was for more than half a century a considerable figure in French philosophy and cultural life.

According to Henri Bergson, who succeeded to Ravaisson's chair in the Académie des Sciences morales et politiques, the ideas put forward in *De l'habitude* left their stamp on an entire generation of philosophers – his own.[50] *De l'habitude* is also a classic of the philosophical movement known as "spiritualism," which may seem to make it an odd companion to *Madame Bovary*. But I am moving too quickly here. Catherine Malabou's preface to the recent republication and translation of *De l'habitude* is clear about the larger stakes of Ravaisson's position:

> There are [her preface begins], in the European philosophical tradition, two basic ways of speaking of habit. Initiated by Aristotle, continued by Hegel and taken up by a certain current of French philosophy (Maine de Biran, Ravaisson, Bergson), the first sees in habit a primary

ontological phenomenon. For beings subject to change, habit is the law of being. Without a general and permanent disposition, a "virtue," which is developed as a result of change, as resistance to this change, the finite being cannot endure, would not have time to live. For such a being, being is fused with the habit of being. The second way, initiated by Descartes and continued by Kant, sees in habit the epitome of inauthenticity, a simulacrum of being, an imitation of virtue. Pure mechanism, routine process, devitalization of sense, habit is the disease of repetition that threatens the freshness of thought and stifles the voice, repeatable but never stale, of the categorical imperative. (vii)

The writings of Pierre Maine de Biran, in particular his *Influence de l'habitude sur la faculté de penser* (1802), were decisive for Ravaisson. Specifically, Ravaisson followed Biran in opposing the effects of repetition on feeling or sensation on the one hand and on movement and perception on the other. In Biran's formulation: "[S]ensation, continued or repeated, fades, is gradually obscured and ends by disappearing without leaving any trace. Repeated movement becomes more precise, more important, and easier"(9). (This is the so-called double law of habit.) Ravaisson followed Biran, too, in holding that habit produces "tendencies" to preserve a sensory equilibrium, or to repeat a movement. But Ravaisson departs from Biran, Clare Carlisle and Mark Sinclair observe, in insisting

> that a single force underlies the double law of habit: [Ravaisson] asserts that continuity or repetition weakens sensibility and excites the power of movement "in the same way, by one and the same cause: the development of an unreflective spontaneity, which breaks into passivity and the organism, and increasingly establishes itself there, beyond, beneath the region of will, personality and consciousness." This spontaneity or desire is at once active and passive, or somehow between these two, and in this way Ravaisson positively deconstructs the distinction between activity and passivity that Biran had tried to maintain. Crucially, he argues that this spontaneity is both intelligent and free even though it has left the sphere of will and reflection – even though it is "blind," as he puts it. It is for this reason that Ravaisson's estimation of

habit is so much more positive than Biran's, who follows his rational-
ist predecessors in identifying intelligence and freedom with reflection
and the will. For Biran, the "blindness" of habit is an obstacle to truth,
whereas for Ravaisson this same fact reveals an intelligence not confined to mental faculties, but dispersed throughout the body and,
indeed, throughout nature as a whole. Similarly, freedom is not confined to the will, and is therefore not annulled by habit, but rather *made
flesh*: as habit progresses, freedom increasingly pervades the body, and
increasingly animates it. (11–12; emphasis in original)

In Ravaisson's words:

> In reflection and will, the end of movement is an idea, an ideal to
> be accomplished: something that should be, that can be and which is
> not yet. It is a possibility to be realized. But as the end becomes fused
> with the movement, and the movement with the tendency, possibility,
> the ideal, is realized in it. The *idea* becomes *being*, the very being of the
> movement and of the tendency that it determines. Habit becomes
> more and more a *substantial idea*. The obscure intelligence that through
> habit comes to replace reflection, this immediate intelligence where
> subject and object are confounded, is a *real* intuition, in which the real
> and the ideal, being and thought are fused together. (55; emphasis in
> original)

All this comes to pass, Ravaisson emphasizes, by imperceptible degrees,
just as it is also by imperceptible degrees that a given habit sometimes
declines, the movements associated with it returning as it does so to the
sphere of the will. "The transition between these two states cannot be
sensed," Ravaisson writes, "its dividing line is everywhere and nowhere.
Consciousness feels itself expire along with the will, and then come back
to life with it, by a gradation and degradation which are continuous; and
consciousness is the first, immediate and unique measure of continuity"
(57). He goes on:

> Not only, then, do the movements that habit gradually removes from
> the will not leave the sphere of intelligence to pass into the grip of a
> blind mechanism, but they also do not withdraw from the same intel-

ligent activity from which they were born. A foreign force [i.e., a merely mechanical one] does not come to direct these movements; it is still the same force that forms their principle, but that, within them, surrenders itself more and more to the attraction of its own thought. It is the same force that, without losing anything of its higher unity in personality, proliferates without being divided; that descends without going under; that dissolves itself, in different ways, into its inclinations, acts and ideas; that is transformed in time, and that is disseminated in space. (57)

A further distinction may be drawn, Ravaisson suggests, between habit so defined and instinct, which he characterizes as "more unreflective, more irresistible, more infallible." But the distinction is not absolute. "Between habit and instinct, between habit and nature, the difference is merely one of degree, and this difference can always be lessened and reduced" (57–9). There follows one of the philosophical high points of the essay as a whole:

> Like effort between action and passion, habit is the dividing line, or the middle term, between will and nature; but it is a moving middle term, a dividing line that is always moving, and which advances by an imperceptible progress from one extremity to the other.
>
> Habit is thus, so to speak, the infinitesimal *differential*, or, the dynamic *fluxion* from Will to Nature. Nature is the *limit* of the regressive movement proper to habit.
>
> Consequently, habit can be considered as a method – as the only real method – for the estimation, by a *convergent infinite* series, of the relation, real in itself but incommensurable in the understanding, of Nature and Will.
>
> In descending gradually from the clearest regions of consciousness, habit carries with it light from those regions into the depths and dark night of nature. Habit is an acquired nature, a *second nature* that has its ultimate ground in primitive nature, but which alone explains the latter to the understanding. It is, finally, a *natured* nature, the product and successive revelation of *naturing* nature. (59; emphasis in original)

Furthermore, Ravaisson argues, the will itself is something more than the simple origin of conscious action. This follows from the need to get past a circular state of affairs in which a subject on the one hand is imagined as becoming aware of the will and its operations only through the overcoming of resistance by an effort and on the other hand becoming aware of resistance only as it is manifested in effort; it therefore follows that there must be "an effortless antecedent tendency, which in its development encounters resistance; and it is at this point that the will finds itself in the self-reflection of activity, and is awakened through effort. [In other words] The will, in general, presupposes a prior inclination – one that is involuntary – in which the subject that develops from it is not yet distinguished from its object." Ravaisson's term for that antecedent tendency is desire; as he also puts it, "Desire is a primordial instinct, in which the goal of the act is fused with the act itself, the idea with the realization, the thought with the spirit of spontaneity; this is the state of nature – it is *nature* itself" (61; emphasis in original).

More than anything else, habit is for Ravaisson both the principle and the sign of the fundamental *continuity* of beings and nature. "The most elementary mode of existence," he states, "with the most perfect organization, is like the final moment of habit, realized and substantiated in space in a physical form. . . . All the way down to the confused and multiple life of the zoophyte, down to plants, even down to crystals, it is thus possible to trace, in this light, the last rays of thought and activity as they are dispersed and dissolved without yet being extinguished, far from any possible reflection, in the vague series of the most obscure instincts" (67). And then:

> The whole series of beings is therefore only the continuous progression of the successive powers of one and the same principle, powers enveloping one another in the hierarchy of the forms of life, powers which develop in the opposite direction within the progression of habit. The lower limit is necessity – Destiny, as might be said, but in the spontaneity of Nature; the higher limit is the Freedom of the understanding. Habit descends from the one to the other; it brings

these contraries together, and in doing so reveals their intimate essence and their necessary connection. (67)

Commenting on these and related passages, the philosopher Dominique Janicaud refers to "the authentically Ravaissonian discovery of the depths of nature as immediate autocausation."[51] As he also says, in Ravaisson's account "spontaneity doesn't cease all at once; its limits are those of nature, or rather of our imagination and our understanding as they seek to represent and understand nature" (47).

Finally, in a remarkable passage on the radical unrepresentability of the absolute continuity of nature, Ravaisson acknowledges that the existence of determinate forms in space – of objects and entities of all kinds – appears to imply discontinuity and limitation. "Nothing, therefore," he writes, "can show that there is an absolute continuity between the limits, and, consequently, that from one extremity of the progression to the other there is the unity of one and the same principle. The continuity of nature is only a possibility, an ideality that cannot be demonstrated in nature itself. But this ideality has its archetype [my translation of "a son type"; the Carlisle-Sinclair version reads "is presented"] in the reality of the progression of habit; it draws its proof from it, by the most powerful of analogies" (65).

My point in introducing *De l'habitude* at this juncture is not positively to suggest that Flaubert read it or that via some other, indirect route it lies behind Canivet's remarks to Homais in the eleventh chapter of part II of *Madame Bovary*. Not that we can be certain that Flaubert was *not* aware of it. But the fact remains that Flaubert never mentions Ravaisson in his correspondence, and there is no indication of his ever having owned a copy of *De l'habitude* – but our knowledge of his personal library is incomplete – or having ordered a copy from elsewhere. Let me state frankly that I half-wish the basic facts were otherwise: it would to my mind make perfect sense for the author of *Madame Bovary* – also of the several versions of *La Tentation de saint Antoine* – to have been familiar with Ravaisson's thought. But this in turn is not to imply that the operation of something like habit that I have been tracking in Flaubert's prose could possibly have *stemmed from* such familiarity. Note, by the way, that Canivet says of himself to Homais, "Je vis tantôt d'une manière, tantôt d'une autre, en philosophe . . ." Is this significant or not? In addition the eminent philosopher Victor Cousin – Ravaisson's chief sponsor early in his career – became Louise Colet's lover in 1839; throughout the years of her relationship with Flaubert he remained loyal to her in important ways; Flaubert knew and indeed approved.[52] Can one go anywhere with this? Probably not, but it at least suggests that Flaubert's and Ravaisson's worlds were not entirely disparate. Finally, perhaps most intriguing, Flaubert, embarked on the extensive studies of ancient Carthage that preceded the writing of *Salammbô*, observed to his friend Ernest Feydeau, "The study of habit leads us to forget the soul."[53] What was he referring to if not to *De l'habitude*? (It seems unlikely that he had nothing specific in mind, but we cannot be certain even of that.) In any case, what I find suggestive – to say the least – is that in Ravaisson's short treatise we have a major philosophical text, by a French contemporary eight years older than Flaubert, that offers a vision of the relation of habit and automatism to intention and consciousness – also, it is important to add, to *nature*, the third key term in Ravaisson's "system" – that may be taken as an anticipatory gloss on or interpretation of those aspects of Flaubert's prose in *Madame Bovary* that I have been placing front and center in this essay, "nature" in that connection comprising the phonemic material at its most sheerly elemental – let us say as a repertory of particular marks and, via the "gueuloir," sounds.[54] Specifically, I understand Ravaisson's insistence on the absolute continuity between will and nature – a continuity mediated by habit as a perpetually moving middle term – to exactly correspond to my claim that in *Madame Bovary* "there is no verbal or phonemic or otherwise proto-linguistic incident, however slight, that can wholly escape the gravitational field of Flaubert's writerly project, just as there are no instances of manifest intention that can wholly escape the implication of a certain automaticity in the mode of their production" (see above). Put slightly differently, if we follow Françoise Gaillard in asking what "theory of the subject" is implied by the sorts of phonemic play that Jean Ricardou drew attention to in his contribution to the 1974 conference and that have been emphasized throughout this essay, one answer, a historically inflected one, might be: the theory of the subject – part of an entire metaphysics – developed by Ravaisson in *De l'habitude*.

I have no idea whether or not the reader of this essay will find the Flaubert/Ravaisson or rather the *Madame Bovary/De l'habitude* association as arresting as I do; at the very least it contextualizes the basic issue of intention versus automaticity and more broadly of will versus nature in a way that suggests that the sorts of observations I have been making in these pages are not simply an artifact of a distinctly modernist or post-modernist (or structuralist or post-structuralist) approach to textuality. More precisely, it may indeed be the case that the observations themselves became entertainable only once certain developments had taken place in the realm of criticism and theory. (And artistic practice: think of Ricar-dou's admiration for Roussel.) But the basic antithesis between intention and automaticity that we have seen at work throughout *Madame Bovary*, and beyond that – more important than that – the mutual implication of the antithetical terms themselves, which is to say the absolute continuity between them (the stronger the one, the stronger the other, is what seems to be the case), turn out to have been anticipated theoretically in a major French philosophical text of 1838, one that we cannot know whether or not Flaubert read but which nevertheless – this is the claim I have been striving toward – cannot safely be ignored by any scholar or critic seeking to take account of the larger historical framework in which *Madame Bovary* came to be written.[55]

7

What makes the Flaubert/Ravaisson association especially resonant for me is that more than twenty years ago I found myself inspired to bring *De l'habitude* to bear on the art of the great French Realist painter (and Flaubert's near-exact contemporary) Gustave Courbet.* This indeed was

---

*   Courbet called his post-1848 practice Realism (with a capital "R"), and I have been faithful to that in my text. References to pictorial or literary realism as such will dispense with the capital.

1   Gustave Courbet, *An After Dinner at Ornans*, oil on canvas, 1848–9. Lille, Musée des Beaux-Arts.

to my mind an important strand of the argument of my book *Courbet's Realism*,[56] albeit it is not one that has been picked up on in the subsequent literature on the painter. Naturally I cannot hope to provide an adequate summary of my account of Courbet's art in the present context. But several points might usefully be made:

First, throughout Courbet's oeuvre one is struck by the importance of a consistent thematics of continuity. This is in stark distinction to the usual account of pictorial realism as being crucially a matter of depicting individual persons and objects in their singularity as well as, even when similar and contiguous, their distinctness and separateness from each other. Beyond this, the basic structural relationship between figures and objects under realism is usually held to be metonymic, in the sense of comprising one thing after another (to adapt Donald Judd's character-

2   Amédée de Lemud, *Master Wolfram*, Lithograph, 1838.

ization of the formal structure of Frank Stella's stripe paintings). And it is also widely assumed that the essence of pictorial realism consists in a relationship of iconic resemblance between the painted image and some portion of the world as the latter presents itself to the sense of sight.

Against these assumptions, I argued in *Courbet's Realism* that in painting after painting by the master of Ornans the separateness and distinctness of persons and objects is overridden, if one can but recognize the fact, by an exactly opposite tendency or rather confluence of tendencies. So for example in the *After Dinner at Ornans* (1848–9; Fig. 1), the canvas that marks his breakthrough to mature achievement (also to his Realism), the four figures seemingly evenly distributed around a table toward the end of a meal (one body after another, so to speak) turn out on closer,

more intent looking to be bound together by a subtle system of grave
and acute axes as well as by a near/far/near/far and side/front/back/
front double syncopation that combine to give the composition a slow
but deeply felt overall rhythm (from left to right and back again) that perfectly suits the heavy, somnolent mood of the depicted scene (the four
men digesting a meal as the three on the left listen to the fourth play the
violin and a dog dozes beneath a chair). Notice, too, how we are not made
to feel that each listener inhabits a separate inner world, as for example
in Amédée de Lemud's ambitious lithograph, *Master Wolfram* (1838; Fig.
2), a source work for the *After Dinner*; rather, one's intuition is of a kind
of continuity or say deep mutual accord among the listeners on that level
also. (As regards technique, the chief operator of effects of continuity in
Courbet's art is his reliance on a dark ground as the visible basis for almost
all his most important paintings. His stake in continuity helps explain why
he went that route, which one might have thought anachronistic by the
1840s; he is, in any case, the last of the major dark-ground painters in the
European tradition.)

In the monumental *A Burial at Ornans* (1849–50; Fig. 3), arguably
Courbet's supreme achievement, the basic structure – not that you would
know it from the secondary literature – is that of a slow, serpentine, mul-
tifigure procession (again, from left to right and back again), organized in
a manner that positively suggests a kind of kinetic if not indeed somatic
continuity from one figure to the next, very much as if a single sustained
powerful impulse were the motivating force behind the procession as a
whole. (There is also a structural knot of some complexity about a third
of the way over from the left, in the neighborhood of the crucifix-bearer,
which I seek to unravel in the chapter on the *Burial* in *Courbet's Realism*.)
For a viewer familiar with Courbet's native Ornans and the Franche-
Comté generally there is also a strong sense of affinity between the
serpentine structure of the composition and the serpentine paths of rivers
such as the Doubs and the Loue as they make their respective ways
through the magnificent, hilly, densely forested terrain; indeed if one
imagines oneself occupying the precise spot from which the painting was
projected (Courbet painted it in Ornans but not, of course, in the open

3　Gustave Courbet, *A Burial at Ornans*, oil on canvas, 1849–50. Paris, Musée d'Orsay.

air looking out at the scene itself), one recognizes that the Loue running through the heart of Ornans lies just beyond and as it were "below" the procession of mourners, and moreover that the *Burial*, like the *After Dinner*, is in effect full of sound, in this case the continuous sound of the water running from right to left over a bed of small stones.

Several other forms of continuity are at work in another stupendous canvas, *The Painter's Studio, Real Allegory Determining a Phase of Seven Years in My Artistic Life* (1854–5; Figs. 4, 5), specifically in the central group comprising Courbet himself seated before a canvas on which he is painting a river landscape, a naked woman standing behind him and holding a length of white drapery to her breast, a small peasant boy standing to the left and looking up at the painter's active right hand, and a white cat playing with a ball at the boy's (and painter's) feet. The standard account of this group, reiterated some years ago by Linda Nochlin, stresses the opposition between the seated, clothed, and active artist and the standing, unclothed, seemingly passive model; Nochlin predictably glosses this as emblematizing a standard masculinist view of the creative process, and no doubt many would agree.[57] But look a bit more closely and the rela-

4   Gustave Courbet, *The Painter's Studio: Real Allegory, Determining a Phase of Seven Years in my Artistic Life*, oil on canvas, 1854–5. Paris, Musée d'Orsay.

tions among the different elements in the group become considerably more interesting: for a start, note the visual "rhyme" between the painter's left shoulder and the woman's hip and buttock; then the off-"rhyme" between the artist's head and her exposed breast; her arms and hands too "repeat" his in the sense that they are engaged in two distinct operations, her left hand (analogous to his palette-hand) holding the cloth to her front and her right hand (higher than her left hand, like his right hand holding a paintbrush relative to the one gripping his palette) raised to her head. One might wish to deny the significance of these analogies, but what about the truly exquisite "rhyme" between the model's forward-tilted neck and head and the painted trees growing from the painted hillside at exactly the same angle? In other words, there is the strongest imaginable suggestion of mutual attunement verging on continuity not only between the painter and the woman but between the latter and the

5   Central group from *The Painter's Studio*.

painting taking shape on the easel. Note too the extreme proximity of the seated painter to his painting – there plainly isn't space enough for his legs not to "enter" or merge with the canvas, with the result that his entire body is encompassed by the canvas in a way that leads one almost to imagine him leaning back against the hillside to the right and extending his right arm and hand further into the picture space in the very act of adding another touch to the painted scene. And as all this takes place one becomes aware that the picture on the easel includes a river flowing directly toward the seated painter – at which point it occurs to one that the white sheet falling from the woman's breast and the discarded clothing at her feet positively invite being seen (metaphorically, but what sort of qualification is that?) as so much falling and eddying water – the white cat, too, takes on the character of a minor cascade – which is to say that the central group, far from exemplifying a culturally stereotypical set of oppositional relations, offers instead a remarkable vision of all but literal continuity among the seated painter, standing woman, picture on the easel, cat, drapery, and clothing, much as if the painter were ultimately to be seen as in the act of painting – as adding the finishing touches to – the central group as a whole. Only the peasant boy seems to take no part in these exchanges; for all his closeness to the canvas he stands apart both from it and from the painter and woman, which in effect makes him "our" representative as we stand looking at the *Painter's Studio* from whatever viewpoint we choose to adopt.

The overarching issue at stake in all this, I contend in *Courbet's Realism*, concerns the antitheatrical aspiration to negate or neutralize what I have called the primordial convention that paintings are made to be beheld, which I see as taking a hyperbolic turn in Courbet's art – the basic idea being that by the late 1840s if not earlier the Diderotian strategy of seeking to accomplish that aim in and through the depiction of figures deeply absorbed in what they were doing, feeling, or thinking and therefore, it appeared, oblivious to being beheld, had reached the limits of its effectiveness. And by hyperbolic turn I mean that in picture after picture by Courbet, starting with the remarkable self-portraits of the 1840s in which his alternative strategy is first given free rein, we find evidence of

6   Gustave Courbet, *The Stonebreakers*, oil on canvas, 1849. Formerly Dresden, Staatliche Gemäldegalerie.

a richly imagined (and no doubt less than fully conscious) attempt to paint himself as if corporeally – all but physically – into the painting being realized under his brush, as if by so doing – had that been literally possible, which of course it was not – there would in the end have been no (first) beholder standing or seated before the canvas for the simple reason that the beholder who had been there, the painter-beholder, was now part of the very fabric of the painting itself. The central group from the *Painter's Studio* is thus exactly what Courbet said it was, a "real allegory" of his basic project (the subtitle of that painting is "Real allegory, determining a phase of seven years in my artistic life"). For its part, another Realist masterpiece, the *Stonebreakers* (1849; Fig. 6), destroyed in World War II, offered still another version of such an attempt, the young man carrying a basket of stones and the older man raising his hammer standing for – more strongly, all but literally embodying – the painter-beholder's left and right hands as they were actively engaged in the making of the painting. That the young man has been depicted largely from the rear and that we see neither of their faces are also pertinent here. Figures viewed from the rear – in other words, figures whose bodily orientation harks back to that of the painter-beholder at work on the canvas – are one of the staples of Courbet's art. Viewed in this light, the *After Dinner* comes close to identifying the painter with the central seated figure of his friend Auguste Marlet lighting his pipe with a burning brand, the action of doing so being in effect a displaced representation of the two-handed action of painting the actual picture.[58] Note too that the *Stonebreakers* invites the viewer to imagine the repetitive sound of the older man's hammer breaking the stones into ever smaller bits.

As a matter of fact it was in the course of researching and writing *Courbet's Realism* that I first encountered *De l'habitude* (initially via Bergson's not wholly reliable discourse mentioned earlier) and was struck by what still seems to me the profound affinity between Ravaisson's metaphysics and Courbet's art. Another aspect of that affinity concerns the primacy of sleep and sleep-related states in Courbet's paintings, a feature first noted years ago by René Huyghe[59] and discussed at length in *Courbet's Realism*. The *After Dinner* is an obvious case in point, with its sleeping dog in the center foreground and the marvelously nuanced figure of Courbet's father in profile slumped in his chair at the left; his left hand still holds his glass (which rests on the table), but apart from that he might well be dozing (his state is at most on the cusp of consciousness). There is something virtually somnambulistic in the movements of the mourners in the right-hand half of the *Burial* as well as in those of boy and man in the *Stonebreakers*, the latter pair in particular conveying the impression of a certain automaticity, a mode of action that while plainly intentional is at the same time repetitive, mechanical, one might say habitual in Ravaisson's construal of the term. (Another way of putting this would be to say all three paintings find means to imply the mutual interpenetration of activity and passivity.) A particularly interesting painting in the latter regard is the sensuous *Sleeping Spinner* (1853; Fig. 7), with its strong suggestion that the female protagonist has fallen asleep in the course of spinning wool, a repetitive action par excellence; passivity, one feels, has the

7   Gustave Courbet, *The Sleeping Spinner*, oil on canvas, 1853. Montpellier, Musée Fabre.

upper hand, but one also intuits that in another moment the spinner
might awaken and the ratio between activity and passivity alter once
more. Indeed the way in which the distaff wound with wool, a traditional
figure for femininity, thrusts into the picture space in a manner analogous
to the phallic painter's brush, suggests a further undoing of opposition,
this time between the female protagonist and the male artist (foreshad-
owing the harmonizing of painter and model in the central group of the
Painter's Studio). All this and much more along these lines, including a consideration of Courbet's landscapes, is developed in *Courbet's Realism*,
though even more than in the case of Flaubert and *Madame Bovary* I stop
well short of proposing that Courbet was aware of Ravaisson's ideas. But
I do suggest

that Courbet's predilection for pictorial structures that evoke an inner continuity between absorptive states and conditions [as in the *After Dinner* and the *Stonebreakers*, for example], and even more his tendency to thematize the mutual interpenetration of action and passivity, will and automatism, have much in common with Ravaisson's views. (According to Francis Wey, Courbet answered criticisms of the smoky tonality of the *After Dinner* by claiming that that was how he saw the scene. "If brighter illumination is necessary," he went on, "I'll think of it and when I see it the thing will be done *without my willing it*" [emphasis added]. And [Courbet's close friend Max] Buchon, in a famous statement, compared Courbet producing paintings to an apple tree producing apples, then glossed this by saying, "As rapidly as Courbet paints, so copiously he sleeps," an equivalence that hints at a mingling of will and automatism where there might seem to be only the latter.) In fact I would go further and propose that Courbet's Realism can usefully be understood in relation to what Ravaisson later called a "spiritualist realism or positivism," as opposed to the usual notions of his art as simply positivist or materialist that have prevailed until now. ("I even make stones think," Courbet boasted to [Théophile] Silvestre.) Finally, I detect an affinity between Ravaisson's speculations on the unrepresentability of the continuity of nature and what has emerged [for example, in my account of the central group in the *Painter's Studio*] as Courbet's determination to represent that continuity by the only means in which it *could* be represented: in figures of ostensible individuation that ultimately demand to be read as I have been reading them in these pages. It's as though the indemonstrable unity of which Ravaisson writes found a further archetype in Courbet's Realist paintings, and that there too what is required of the interpreter, if their metaphysical meaning is to be understood, is a capacity for discerning [in this case] visual analogies. (183–4)

To say this, however, is not to imply that the analogies are fundamentally symbolic or intellectual. On the contrary, they are as sensuously immediate as any other aspect of the paintings, as in the works we have con-

8   Gustave Courbet, *The Wave*, oil on canvas, 1869. Staatliche Museen zu Berlin, National-galerie.

sidered (the notion of "real allegory" says as much), or to take another, somewhat different example, as in *The Wave* (1869; Fig. 8) in Berlin, with its blatantly material, masterfully worked picture surface and, on the plane of depiction (not that the two can be separated in the viewer's experience), its heavy mass of green-blue and white water about to smash itself on the pebbly beach in the near foreground, as if in response to – as if called up by – the painter-beholder's sustained effort to paint himself into the canvas before him. The "pull" of the distant horizon belongs to this structure as well. Also characteristic of Courbet's particular vision are the two smallish rocks in the left foreground, just far enough apart to enforce a sense of their separateness, which as one contemplates them appear virtually in conversation with each other.

So much, at the present juncture, for Courbet and Ravaisson. What if anything does the above tell us about Courbet and Flaubert?

Nothing hard and fast, is the answer. For one thing, there is a basic difference in attitude to be taken into account, namely, that Courbet embraced the designation "realist" (with a capital "R") while Flaubert never ceased to resist it. For another, a related point, nothing in Courbet's letters or recorded utterances matches Flaubert's anguished declarations of the pursuit of stylistic perfection, and in fact there is nothing in Courbet's practice – it is hard to see how there could be anything in the practice of painting generally – comparable to the "gueuloir." Finally, it is far from obvious that the new, more radical, but also conspicuously impersonal "appearance of intention" that Maupassant noted in Flaubert's prose is the equivalent of what I have tried to show was Courbet's imaginative projection of himself in the act of painting into works such as the *After Dinner*, *Stonebreakers*, and *Sleeping Spinner*, not to mention the *Painter's Studio*, in which he turns up in propria persona. Nevertheless, if I am right in my claims about them both, something like a Ravaissonian conception of habit, or say a Ravaissonian intuition of the continuity between will and nature as mediated by habit, plays a role – different in the two cases – in Courbet's Realist paintings on the one hand and Flaubert's breakthrough novel, itself (pace Flaubert) a masterpiece of literary realism, on the other. Again, this is not to suggest that *De l'habitude* in any sense lies behind their respective achievements. But it is at least to insist that that extremely interesting text be counted among the significant cultural markers of the period between the heyday of Romanticism in France and the emergence of artistic and literary realism in the late 1840s and 1850s.[60]

8

A half-dozen diverse topics bearing on these issues are worth pursuing briefly, after which I shall conclude by saying something further about Flaubert and Proust.

The first, a huge topic that I can only indicate in summary fashion, concerns the clear echoes in Ravaisson's conception of habit of German idealist aesthetics during the years immediately before and shortly after 1800, in the wake of Immanuel Kant's major treatises and in particular *The Critique of Judgment* of 1790. Above all it is the definition of habit as the "mediating" term between will and nature, freedom and destiny, consciousness and matter, as well as the description of it as both active and passive, spontaneous and immediate, that link Ravaisson's notion to theorizations of the function of beauty from Kant onward, especially as put forward in Schelling's influential if also extraordinarily difficult writings of the first decade of the nineteenth century, *The System of Transcendental Idealism* (1800), *The Philosophy of Art* (delivered as lectures in 1802–3 and 1804–5, but not published until much later), and the *System of the Whole of Philosophy and of Naturphilosophie in Particular* (1804). The last part of the first of these texts is devoted to art, and centers on questions of the relation of consciousness and its opposite, as in the claim that in every work of art "the basic character of the work of art is that of an *unconscious infinity* [synthesis of nature and freedom]. Besides what he has put into the work with manifest intention, the artist seems instinctively, as it were, to have depicted therein an infinity, which no finite understanding is capable of developing to the full. . . . [Every true work of art] is capable of being expounded *ad infinitum*, as though it contained an infinity of purposes, while yet one is never able to say whether this infinity has lain within the artist himself, or resides only in the work of art."[61] The concomitant claim by Ravaisson that habit is a second nature likewise carries echoes of Friedrich Schiller's definition of beauty in his *Letters on the Aesthetic Education of Man* of 1795, one of the foundational texts on art of the entire modern period. This is not the place for even the sketchiest attempt to expand on these associations. But if the basic project of the present essay is found persuasive, they open a surprising perspective on the respective achievements of two of the foremost figures in French literature and painting of the mid- and later nineteenth century. In this connection it is intriguing to find Bergson, in "The Life and Work of

Ravaisson," stressing the affinity between the young Ravaisson's interest in Italian Renaissance art, in particular Leonardo da Vinci, and his early work on Aristotle's metaphysics, and then going on to state: "The whole philosophy of Ravaisson springs from the idea that art is a figured metaphysics, that metaphysics is a reflection of art, and that it is the same intuition, variously applied, which makes the profound philosopher and the great artist. Ravaisson took possession of himself, became master of his thought and his pen the day that this identity revealed itself clearly to his mind" (231). This is, I need hardly add, one of the fundamental tenets of Schelling's aesthetics, indeed of his philosophy generally.[62] Regrettably, Bergson does not pursue the subject further.

A second topic is most directly broached by way of Charles Baudelaire's brilliant aperçu in his essay on *Madame Bovary* to the effect that Emma possessed a range of distinctly masculine virtues: for example, it is she, alone of the characters in the novel, who possesses the supreme Baudelairean virtue of imagination; who is capable of sudden actions, quick decisions, and the "mystical fusion of reasoning and passion which characterizes men created for action"; and whose desire to dominate and to seduce can be summed up in the highly charged Baudelairean term "dandysme."[63] In fact Baudelaire went considerably further, writing: "It only remained for the author, to accomplish the whole of his tour de force, to divest himself (as much as possible) of his sex and make himself a woman. The result is a marvel; it's that, despite all his zeal as an actor [i.e., for all his desire not to give himself away], he could not not infuse virile blood into his creature's veins, and that Madame Bovary, in everything about her that is the most energetic and the most ambitious – also the most full of dreams – Madame Bovary remains a man. Like Pallas issuing fully armed from the forehead of Zeus, this bizarre androgyne has kept all the seductions of a virile soul in a charming feminine body" (647). Considerably more could be said in this vein,[64] but it is pertinent to the Flaubert/Courbet question that in my book on the latter I make much of what I call "Courbet's 'Femininity,'" by which I meant Courbet's tendency to "project" his activity as a painter into female figures in works

9   Gustave Courbet, *The Wheat Sifters*, oil on canvas, 1854. Nantes, Musée des Beaux-Arts.

such as the *Sleeping Spinner*, in which (as mentioned above) the brush/distaff is at once phallic and distinctly "feminine";[65] the coloristically daring *Wheat Sifters* (1854; Fig. 9), a canvas featuring two women farm laborers in a sunlit interior, in which Courbet's pictorial project as I have summarized it is expressed in almost every detail (typically, the principal sifter has been depicted from the rear); and *The Source* (1868; Fig. 10), a seated nude seen from the rear in a forest setting which in effect condenses in a single female figure the central group in the *Painter's Studio* (including the painting on the easel, which finds its equivalent in the reflection of the seated woman in the water). The conspicuous dissolving or transcending of gender oppositions that this entails is not exactly

10   Gustave Courbet, *The Source*, oil on canvas, 1868. Paris, Musée Orsay.

the same as the author's identification with his female protagonist that Baudelaire singled out as crucial to Flaubert's achievement in *Madame Bovary*, but the two phenomena are clearly related to one another in important respects. And another point: it speaks volumes about the peculiar limitation of the nineteenth-century discourse on pictorial realism that Baudelaire, the subtlest art critic of his generation, could never have recognized in Courbet's paintings the sort of complexities with respect to gender he so keenly discerned in Flaubert's novel: for him, the notion of realism in connection with painting meant the death of the imagination, period. (There was for Baudelaire no essential difference between Courbet's Realist paintings and photography.) Put another way, pictorial realism could only be understood by him as requiring the sacrifice of truly artistic faculties in the interest of the sheerest materialism. But of course the "imaginative" aspects of Courbet's art were to go unrecognized for a long time to come.

The issue of materialism in the art of Flaubert and Courbet is not exhausted by these considerations. The most insightful critical text as regards Flaubert is Charles Du Bos's "Sur le milieu intérieur" of 1921. I earlier quoted Du Bos's subtle observations on what he called the lack of "air" in Flaubert's prose, the sense in which the blank spaces between words were only nominally blank, or as he also put it, the way in which Flaubert filled up every hole, every fissure, with verbal material. In this connection, too, I cited Proust's admiration for "those heavy materials which Flaubert's sentences lift and let fall with the intermittent noise of an excavator." But it is Du Bos who makes the imaginative leap of associating this aspect of Flaubert's prose with what might be called the latter's primordial bodily being. (Du Bos is writing phenomenological criticism *avant la lettre*, as it seems to me.) Starting out from the biologist Claude Bernard's notion of "le milieu intérieur," Du Bos proceeds to describe that "milieu" in the young Flaubert's case as

> a mass imposing in its volume, but undifferentiated and as if torpid, and which reveals on close examination thousands of infinitesimal movements all of which react on the whole mass: it is a stretched-out animal in which can be observed the blind agitation of all the smaller animal cells that compose it. *Mens agitat molem* [the mind informs the mass]; but in this case, only the *moles*, at the beginning, declares its presence; the *mens* is still too trapped, too engulfed. No trace of those accents, those differences of relief, those emerging directions of flows of water by virtue of which a future genius indicates the first lineaments of his future geographical map. And the mass itself, in the case

of Flaubert, is enveloped by dense fog: to pierce it will be necessary for him at every moment to deploy forces out of all proportion to the results to be obtained.[66]

Flaubert's task as a writer, as he struggled to realize his outsize ambition, was to make something positive out of this essentially negative condition. It is in this light, Du Bos suggests, that we should understand the "imperishable last page" of the 1875 version of *La Tentation de saint Antoine*, with its anguished (or perhaps triumphant) cry, "Pénétrer chaque atome, descendre jusqu'au fond de la matière, être la matière!" ["Penetrate every atom, descend to the very depths of matter, be matter!"].[67] Following which Du Bos cites a famous passage from an 1852 letter to Louise Colet in which Flaubert, having begun work on *Madame Bovary*, speaks of having within him two "bonshommes": one who loves lyricism in all its excessiveness; and another "who excavates and digs through the true as best he can, who loves to reveal the small fact as powerfully as the great fact, who would make you feel almost *materially* the things he depicts."[68] Du Bos comments, "it is only the 'almost' that could be deleted: Flaubert is a genius of materiality; nothing surpasses the continuity and the power of the thoughts that he exerts."[69] As he also remarks, "this power of identification with matter, it is precisely that, at the beginning, that prevented Flaubert from emerging; further on he would be able to use it, at first he was only its prey."[70] But Flaubert did eventually learn to utilize it, nowhere more tenaciously, Du Bos implies, than in the compacted, "air"-less texture of his mature writing.[71]

I find all this acute, and would only add, first, that nothing would have been more natural than for Flaubert to have included *De l'habitude* among his copious preparatory reading for the first *Tentation de saint Antoine*, and second, that I have no difficulty imagining Courbet – an intensely "bodily" painter, as *Courbet's Realism* seeks to demonstrate – endorsing Saint Anthony's sentiment ("I even make stones think," I have quoted him as saying). Such a natural propensity in both writer and painter would have inclined each to a Ravaissonian vision of reality.[72]

A fourth topic takes off from a surprising observation in the essay that provoked Proust's marvelous essay of 1920, the eminent critic Albert

Thibaudet's "Sur le style de Flaubert" (1919). This is where Thibaudet launched his critique of Flaubert as a writer who regularly made grammatical mistakes, who in other respects as well fell short of complete mastery of French, and whose language and above all whose syntax "as the Goncourts point out . . . has nothing impulsive, nervous, or daring about it."[73] In this connection he writes:

> One day, I thought I saw a figure for Flaubert in doctor Larivière [a more eminent personage than Canivet, who is sent for when Emma is on her deathbed]. Much more today I would see him in Binet instead. In the assiduous practice of turnery, Binet has found peace and a certain discipline to be at his disposal. He turns like Flaubert writes. It takes talent, vocation, he has them and adds to them thanks to a continual effort. But Flaubert does not reach Binet's level. The practice of turnery for Binet is a pleasure in itself that is enough to provide him with a complete reason to live. It is of no use to his satisfaction that Monsieur Homais praises his products in the *Fanal de Rouen* and lets them be admired by a wide audience. Flaubert on the contrary would not turn anything if he did not have the *Fanal* and Monsieur Homais. Intelligent destiny, by the way, placed Monsieur Homais at his side under the name Maxime Du Camp.[74]

This seems absurdly harsh, as regards both Flaubert and Du Camp, but the comparison with Binet and his dedication to his lathe is not therefore an irrelevant one, as is shown by the frequency with which it has been advanced by subsequent commentators.[75] Here I will simply point to one aspect of Binet's activity that bears on the argument of the present essay (and to various observations by Du Bos and Proust cited above) – the way in which the "ronflement monotone" (186) ["monotonous drone" (113)] of his lathe can be heard throughout Yonville, in effect filling the space (one might almost say the "air") of the town with meaningless sound. It may be still another point in common between Flaubert and Courbet that (as was mentioned earlier) the *After Dinner* is to be imagined filled with the sound of violin-playing, the *Stonebreakers* with that of the fall of the older man's hammer, and that were one actually standing where the *Burial* positions its viewer one would hear the murmur of the Loue flowing over its bed – by no means the only evocations of sustained or repetitive sound in Courbet's oeuvre.

A fifth topic concerns the notion of realism as applied to *Madame Bovary*, or rather as that subject is treated in a recent essay by Jonathan Culler, who focuses on various passages that seem to veer between an obvious *effet de réel* and what Culler describes as "a certain surreal, hallucinatory effect."[76] "In the famous fiacre scene [when Emma and Léon make love in a closed fiacre that wanders as if distractedly all over Rouen]," he writes, "the multiplication of place names – streets and neighborhoods of Rouen – starts as referentiality that connotes the real, but as the names proliferate, they become hallucinatory, incantatory:

> Elle [la voiture] revint; et alors, sans parti pris ni direction, au hasard, elle vagabonda. On la vit à Saint-Pol, à Lescure, au mont Gargan, à la Rouge-Mare, et place du Gaillard-Bois; rue Maladrerie, rue Dinanderie, devant Saint-Romain, Saint-Vivien, Saint-Maclou, Saint-Nicaise, – devant la Douane, – à la basse Vieille-Tour, aux Trois-Pipes et au Cimetière Monumental. (372)

> There it turned back; and from then on it wandered at random, without apparent goal. It was seen at Saint-Pol, at Lescure, at Mont-Gargan, at Rouge-Mare and the Place du Gaillardbois; in the Rue Maladrerie, the Rue Dinanderie, and in front of one church after another – Saint-Romain, Saint-Vivien, Saint-Maclou, Saint-Nicaise; in front of the customs house, at the Basse Vieille-Tour, at Trois Pipes, and at the Cimetière Monumental. (279)

"Referentiality or *effet de réel* so hyperbolic as to become hallucinatory" (695)? The question is apt, so long as we recognize that what Culler calls hallucination is tantamount to an obscure perception of the sense-defying relations among the various phonemes the passage comprises, as each new cluster – as if in accord with a logic that never quite discloses itself – appears to call up successor phonemes and recall previous ones, culminating in the hyphened-off balance-point "devant la Douane" and then

the resonant sequence "Vieille-Tour," "Trois-Pipes," and "Cimetière Monumental." (Note, by the way, the succession of *v*'s that punctuates the
passage from start to finish.)[77]

Finally, my argument in this essay raises the further question of the
relation, on a micro-textual level, of *Madame Bovary* to Flaubert's other
mature works – *Salammbô*, *L'Education sentimentale*, the final version of *La
Tentation de saint Antoine*, *Trois Contes*, and *Bouvard et Pécuchet*. This is a
much larger topic than I can begin to engage with here, but I will make
two brief assertions. First, although the practice of the "gueuloir" –
reading his sentences in a loud voice as a means of testing them against
an inner ideal – continued throughout his career, the particular marriage
of intention and automatism, will and nature, that we have discovered at
work throughout *Madame Bovary* is specific to that text. By this I do not
mean that nothing remotely like it can be found in various passages elsewhere in Flaubert's oeuvre. My point is rather that it would be impossible to generate apropos Flaubert's other books the sorts of commentary
and debate to which the writing of *Madame Bovary* gave rise long before
I became intrigued by the question of how in relation to the latter the
"gueuloir" actually worked. And second, in the extraordinary "historical"
novel set in ancient Carthage that immediately followed *Madame Bovary*,
the *sui generis Salammbô*, composed between 1858 and 1862, what we find
almost everywhere on a micro-textual level is a forest, one might say an
army, of alliterations, assonances, and repetitions at least as dense and
challenging to negotiate as anything we have noted in its great predeces-
sor (indeed often more dense and challenging) but now without the slightest intimation at any juncture that that density is other than intended,
willed, organized as such – in short, other than "voulu." The result is a
significantly different experience of reading, of attending at once to the
writing itself and to the extravagantly sensuous "reality" it seeks to evoke,
than the one I have tried to evoke in these pages. A separate essay, "Willing
Salammbô," seeks to spell this out.

★

9

Let me bring this essay to a close by returning briefly to Proust in "A propos du 'style' de Flaubert." Earlier I quoted Proust's writing: "Yet we love those heavy materials which Flaubert's sentences lift and let fall again with the intermittent noise of an excavator. For if, as has been written, Flaubert's lamp at night served seafarers as a lighthouse, one might also say that the sentences emitted through his 'gueuloir' had the regular rhythm of the machines that are used for clearing away spoil. Fortunate those who are alive to this obsessive rhythm" – at which point there appears a semi-colon, then:

> but those who are unable to rid themselves of it, who, whatever the topic they have to deal with, remain subject to the master's scansion and invariably produce 'Flaubertese,' are like those unfortunates of German folklore condemned to live forever tied to the clapper of a bell. And so, where Flaubert-intoxication is concerned, I cannot recommend authors too strongly to the purgative and exorcizing merits of pastiche. When we have just finished a book, not only would we like to go on living with its characters, with Mme de Beauséant [*Père Goriot*] or with Frédéric Moreau [*L'Education sentimentale*], but also our inner voice, disciplined all the time we have been reading to follow the rhythm of a Balzac or a Flaubert, would like to go on speaking as they do. We need to give it its head for a moment, to allow the pedal to sustain the sound, that is, to produce a voluntary pastiche so that afterward we can become original once more and not produce involuntary pastiche all our lives. Voluntary pastiche we produce in a quite spontaneous way; it can well be imagined that when, in the old days, I wrote a pastiche – execrable, as it happens – of Flaubert, I had not asked myself whether the melody I could hear inside me depended on the repetition of imperfects or present participles. Otherwise I should never have been able to transcribe it. It is an opposite labor I have accomplished today in seeking hastily to note down these few peculiarities of Flaubert's style. Our minds are never satisfied unless they can provide a clear analysis of what they had first produced unconsciously, or a living recreation of what they had first patiently analyzed. (268–9)[78]

This is to say that in the course of reading certain strong texts by Balzac or Flaubert (for example), a reader who is also a writer risks aquiring a habit of not only assenting to but also in a sense inwardly continuing or repeating those authors' characteristic modes of making prose (including, in Flaubert's case, a certain repetitive rhythm) and that one way of curing oneself of this tendency so as not to go on to produce an inadvertent pastiche of the authors in question is to shift the register toward conscious intention by a practice of deliberate or willed pastiche. Proust further specifies that the practice of intentional pastiche can be, indeed must be, "spontaneous," i.e., not the result of conscious stylistic analysis of the "model" text – an unexpected distinction that in effect treats intentional pastiche as perhaps closer to the "model" (as more "mimetic," closer to "suggestion") than we might imagine it to be. In other words, we are dealing here with still another, a distinctly Proustian version of, antithesis *but also continuity* between intention and automatism such as was theorized by Ravaisson and, after a delay of about a decade, was actualized in the *After Dinner, Stonebreakers, Burial,* and other Realist canvases by Courbet and in *Madame Bovary* by Flaubert (much less than a decade if we see this as beginning in Courbet's self-portraits of the 1840s, as in fact we should).

As Proust implies, he had some years earlier deliberately pasticdied Flaubert along with other well-known writers: Balzac, Henri de Régnier, the Goncourts in their *Journal,* Jules Michelet, Emile Faguet, Ernest Renan, Chateaubriand, and (at greatest length) Saint-Simon. All these are presented as treating in their characteristic manners the same subject, the so-called "Affaire Lemoine," a real-life crime in which a con man named Henri Lemoine claimed to have discovered the secret of manufacturing diamonds from coal, and persuaded various persons, including Sir Julius Werner, president of De Beers, to invest in his scheme; eventually Lemoine was found out and in 1909 was sentenced to six years in prison. Proust's pastiche of Flaubert, about 750 words in length, begins:

> La chaleur devenait étouffante, une cloche tinta, des tourterelles s'envolèrent, et, les fenêtres ayant été fermées sur l'ordre du président, une odeur de poussière se répandit.[79]

The heat had become stifling, a bell chimed, some turtledoves took flight, and, the windows having been closed by order of the presiding magistrate, a smell of dust spread.[80]

It is hard to imagine a single sentence more packed with alliteration of the sort we have analyzing: "chaleur" is immediately (doubly) picked up by "cloche"; the *d* of "devenait" is followed by the same letter in "ordre," "président," "odeur,"and "répandit"; the *t*'s of "étouffante" are immediately echoed by "tinta" and "tourterelles," not to mention "fenêtres" a little way further on; the double *f* of "étouffante" is recalled by "fenêtres" and "fermées"; and the *p* of "président" is immediately seconded by "poussière" and, again, "répandit." (The "en" and "an" sounds are also prominent.) There are also, of course, two *v*'s, in "devenait" and "s'envolèrent." The second sentence continues in the same vein:

Il était vieux, avec un visage de pitre, une robe trop étroite pour sa corpulence, des prétentions à l'esprit; et ses favoris égaux, qu'un reste de tabac salissait, donnaient à toute sa personne quelque chose de décoratif et de vulgaire. (269)

He was old, with a clown's face, wore a gown too narrow for his girth, and had pretensions to wit; his twin sideburns, which a trace of tobacco stained, gave something ornamental and vulgar to his entire person. (17)

Four *v*'s, including the final word; *p*'s and *t*'s galore; another *f* in "favoris"; "salissait" with its paired *s*-sounds looking forward to "personne" just a few words later. Then:

Comme la suspension d'audience se prolongeait, des intimités s'ébauchèrent; pour entrer en conversation, les malins se plaignaient à haute voix du manque d'air, et, quelqu'un ayant dit reconnaître le ministre de l'Intérieur dans un monsieur qui sortait, un réactionnaire soupira: "Pauvre France!" (269)

Since the adjournment of the hearing was prolonged, private exchanges started up; to enter into conversation, the irritable ones complained out loud about the lack of air, and, when someone said he had recognized the Minister of the Interior as the gentleman who was going out, a reactionary sighed, "Poor France!" (17–18)

Here too *p*'s and *t*'s play a prominent role, along with *s*'s; the letter *m* suddenly comes to the fore in "malins," "manque," "ministre," and "monsieur"; the words "à haute voix" give us another *v* as does the final phrase, "Pauvre France," the framing of which by quotation marks – also the capitalization of both words – has the effect of thematizing *p* and *f* across the entire opening of the pastiche (cf. the *c*'s and *b*'s in the description of Charles Bovary's "casquette" – "pauvre chose" – in chapter one of *Madame Bovary*, singled out by Ricardou in his talk at Cerisy). All this is to say nothing of the profusion of "en," "on," and "an" sounds. I stop short, barely, of attributing significance for the argument of this essay to the phrase "manque d'air," not to mention "à haute voix."[81]

I could go on – the next sentences are almost irresistible – but I take it the point is clear. Proust in his pastiche implicitly recognized and placed center stage not only the use of the imperfect and present participle and the conjunction "et" that he would later brilliantly discuss, but also – unmistakably – the densely repetitive phonemic micro-structure of Flaubert's prose in *Madame Bovary* that has been the focus of my reflections in this essay.[82] Whether or not Proust in his capacity as critical analyst (and what a critical analyst!) ever specifically sought to understand that micro-structure in its own right beyond noting the obsessive rhythmic effects to which it gave rise is still another open question.*

---

*   Nothing could be more reassuring than to have Proust on one's side, so to speak. But there is another notable figure whom I would like to enlist among my supporters – Friedrich Nietzsche. At any rate, I recently was struck by the following paragraph in his late text, *The Case of Wagner* (1888):

> For the moment I am only going to look at the question of *style*. – What is the hallmark of all *literary* decadence? The word becomes sovereign and jumps out of the sentence, the sentence reaches out and blots out the meaning of the page, the page comes to life at the expense of the whole – the whole is not whole any more. But this is the image of every decadent style: there is always an anarchy of the atom, disintegration

CODA:
EMMA'S FUNERAL

Emma is dead. The church service is over and the funeral procession begins its undulating, slow-moving journey to the graveyard. The description of the journey and the burial takes up fewer than two pages in the Livre de Poche edition of *Madame Bovary*:

> On se tenait aux fenêtres pour voir passer le cortège. Charles, en avant, se cambrait la taille. Il affectait un air brave et saluait d'un signe ceux qui, débouchant des ruelles ou des portes, se rangeaient dans la foule.
>
> Les six hommes, trois de chaque côté, marchaient au petit pas et en haletant un peu. Les prêtres, les chantres et les deux enfants de choeur récitaient le *De Profundis*; et leurs voix s'en allaient sur la campagne, montant et s'abaissant avec des ondulations. Parfois ils disparaissaient aux détours du sentier; mais la grande croix d'argent se dressait toujours entre les arbres.

---

of the will, "freedom of the individual," morally speaking, – or, expanded into a political theory, "*equal* rights for all." Life, *equal* vitality, the vibration and exuberance of life pushed back into the smallest structures, all the rest *impoverished* of life. Paralysis everywhere, exhaustion, numbness *or* hostility and chaos: both becoming increasingly obvious the higher you climb in the forms of organization. The whole does not live at all any more: it is cobbled together, calculated, synthetic, an artifact. (Friedrich Nietzsche, "The Case of Wagner," in *The Anti-Christ, Ecce Homo, Twilight of the Idols and Other Writings*, ed. Aaron Ridley and Judith Norman, trans. Judith Norman [Cambridge and New York, 2005], 245. Emphasis in original.)

My impulse, on reading this, was at once to think of *Madame Bovary*, perceived from a distinctly unsympathetic angle of vision. And just five pages later there occurs the remark that "every single Wagnerian heroine becomes pretty much indistinguishable from Madame Bovary! – which lets you see that Flaubert *could* have translated his heroine into Scandinavian or Carthaginian [a reference, obviously, *to Salammbô*, also in Nietzsche's sights] and, properly mythologized, offered her to Wagner as a libretto." Followed by: "Yes, Wagner is only interested [in] the same problems that interest the little Parisian

Les femmes suivaient, couvertes de mantes noires à capuchon rabattu; elles portaient à la main un gros cierge qui brûlait, et Charles se sentait défaillir à cette continuelle répétition de prières et de flambeaux, sous ces odeurs affadissantes de cire et de soutane. Une brise fraîche soufflait, les seigles et les colzas verdoyaient, des gouttelettes de rosée tremblaient au bord du chemin, sur les haies d'épines. Toutes sortes de bruits joyeux emplissaient l'horizon: le claquement d'une charrette roulant au loin dans les ornières, le cri d'un coq qui se répétait ou la galopade d'un poulain que l'on voyait s'enfuir sous les pommiers. Le ciel pur était tacheté de nuages roses; des fumignons bleuâtres se rabattaient sur les chaumières couvertes d'iris; Charles, en passant, reconnaissait les cours. Il se souvenait de matins comme celui-ci, où, après avoir visité quelque malade, il en sortait, et retournait vers elle.

Le drap noir, semé de larmes blanches, se levait de temps à autre en découvrant la bière. Les porteurs fatigués se ralentissaient, et elle avançait par saccades continues, comme une chaloupe qui tangue à chaque flot.

---

decadents these days, just writ large" (250; emphasis in original). And in "Nietzsche Contra Wagner" (1888):

> Nowadays I avail myself of this primary distinction concerning artists of every type: is it *hatred* of life or *superabundance* of life that has become creative here? In Goethe, for instance, superabundance has become creative, in Flaubert it is hatred: Flaubert, a new edition of Pascal, but as an artist, based on the instinctive judgment: 'Flaubert est toujours *haïssable*, l'homme n'est rien, *l'oeuvre est tout*' . . . He tortured himself when he wrote, just as Pascal tortured himself when he thought – they both felt unegoistic . . . "Selflessness" – that principle of decadence, the will to the end in art as in morality. (Ibid., 272; emphasis in original.)

What interests me, of course, is less the negative judgment than its grounds, above all the notion that Flaubert's style betrays "an anarchy of the atom" (inspired phrase!) such that "Life, *equal* vitality, the vibration and exuberance of life [are] pushed back into the smallest structures," which would be one way, unexpected but brilliant, of characterizing the phonemic play that has been my concern throughout this essay.

On arriva.

Les hommes continuèrent jusqu'en bas, à une place dans le gazon où la fosse était creusée.

On se rangea tout autour; et, tandis que le prêtre parlait, la terre rouge, rejetée sur les bords, coulait par les coins sans bruit, continuellement.

Puis, quand les quatre cordes furent disposées, on poussa la bière dessus. Il la regarda descendre. Elle descendait toujours.

Enfin on entendit un choc; les cordes en grinçant remontèrent. Alors Bournisien prit la bêche que lui tendait Lestiboudois; de sa main gauche, tout en aspergeant de la droite, il poussa vigoureusement une large pelletée; et le bois du cercueil, heurté par les cailloux, fit ce bruit formidable qui nous semble être le retentissement de l'éternité.

L'ecclésiastique passa le goupillon à son voisin. C'était M. Homais. Il le secoua gravement, puis le tendit à Charles, qui s'affaissa jusqu'aux genoux dans la terre, et il en jetait à pleines mains tout en criant: "Adieu!" Il lui envoyait des baisers; il se traînait vers la fosse pour s'y engloutir avec elle.

On l'emmena; et il ne tarda pas à s'apaiser, éprouvant peut-être, comme tous les autres, la vague satisfaction d'en avoir fini. (486–8)

People stood at their windows to watch the procession. Charles, at the head, held himself very straight. He put on a brave front and nodded to those who came out from the lanes and the doorways to join the crowd.

The six men, three on each side, walked with short steps, panting a little. The priests, the cantors and the two choir-boys recited the *De Profundis*; and their voices carried over the fields, rising and falling in waves. Sometimes they disappeared from view at a twist of the path; but the great silver cross was always visible, high up among the trees.

At the rear were the women, in their black cloaks with turned-down hoods; each of them carried a thick lighted candle; and Charles felt himself overcome amidst this endless succession of prayers and lights, these cloying odors of wax and cassocks. A cool breeze was blowing, the rye and the colza were sprouting green; dewdrops shimmered on the thorn hedges along the road. All kinds of joyous sounds filled the air – the rattle of a jolting cart in distant ruts, the repeated crowing of a cock, the thudding of a colt as it bolted off under the apple trees. The pure sky was dappled with rosy clouds; wisps of bluish smoke trailed down over the thatched cottages, their roofs abloom with iris. Charles recognized each farmyard as he passed. He remembered leaving them on mornings like this after making sick calls, on his way back to where she was.

The black pall, embroidered with white tears, flapped up now and again, exposing the coffin beneath. The tired pallbearers were slowing down, and the bier moved forward in a series of jerks, like a boat pitching at every wave.

They reached the cemetery.

The pallbearers continued on to where the grave had been dug in the turf.

Everyone stood around it; and as the priest spoke, the reddish earth, heaped up on the edges, kept sliding down at the corners, noiselessly and continuously.

Then, when the four ropes were in position, the coffin was pushed onto them. He watched it go down. It went down and down.

Finally there was a thud, and the ropes creaked as they came back up. Then Bournisien took the shovel that Lestiboudois held out to him. With his left hand – all the while sprinkling holy water with his right – he vigorously pushed in a large spadeful of earth; and the stones striking the wood of the coffin made that awesome sound that seems to us like the very voice of eternity.

The priest passed his sprinkler to the person beside him. It was Homais. He shook it gravely, then handed it to Charles, who sank on his knees in the pile of earth and threw it into the grave in handfuls, crying, "*Adieu!*" He blew her kisses, and dragged himself toward the grave as though to be swallowed up in it with her.

They led him away, and he soon grew calmer – vaguely relieved, perhaps, like everyone else that it was all over. (382–4)

It is at once clear, I think, that the sorts of phonemic relationships I have been stressing are intermittently in evidence. But my interest in the scene of Emma's burial has another basis.

In a note to the above passage in the same edition, Jacques Neefs cites a letter from Flaubert to Louise Colet dated 6 June 1853, the day before the burial of one Mme Pouchet, in which the author, well embarked on his novel, remarks that he is certain "that tomorrow's will be a somber spectacle and that the poor scholar [the widower] will be wretched. Perhaps I'll find something there for my *Bovary*" (488n1).[83]

There is no reason to doubt that he did just that. But there may be another, very different term of reference for Emma's funeral – Gustave Courbet's modern *tableau historique* of 1849–50, *A Burial at Ornans*. At any rate, that is the premise, the suggestion, of this coda: while acknowledging the lack of corroborating evidence (a letter, for example, actually mentioning the *Burial*), and bearing in mind the fact that Flaubert was traveling in the Middle East with his friend Maxime Du Camp when the *Burial* was first revealed to the Parisian public at the Salon of 1850–51, I want to suggest that Flaubert during the years of his labors on *Madame Bovary* could not have been unaware of Courbet's canvas, the single most ambitious and controversial painting by a French artist of the entire decade. This is obviously not the place for a full discussion of Courbet's intentions in that remarkable work; I analyze the latter in detail in *Courbet's Realism*, focusing in particular on its "structure of beholding," which is to say on the various means and devices by which an extremely precise set of relationships involving what might be called the "beholder function" is put in place by the painting itself. But what at least should be noted here is that the *Burial* is a monumental work, roughly eight feet high by just under twenty-two feet wide, depicting a funeral at the so-called new cemetery in Courbet's native Ornans, a town on the Loue just a short distance from Besançon in the Franche-Comté. It was painted in Ornans during the winter of 1849–50, and was exhibited in Paris in the Salon of 1850–51 and again in Courbet's own Pavillon du Réalisme, coinciding with the Exposition Universelle of 1855. The critical response in

Paris when it was first shown was overwhelmingly negative,[84] but in the course of the 1850s it nevertheless imposed itself as the central work of pictorial Realism, a term coined by Courbet's champion, the novelist and critic Champfleury (Jules Husson), and accepted by the painter. Flaubert himself, as is well known, resisted the notion of realism as applied to his own literary work. What he meant by this, presumably, is that he did not want his writing and in particular *Madame Bovary* to be confused with the novels and more broadly the literary aims of would-be novelist successors to Balzac such as Champfleury or Edmond Duranty (editor of a short-lived journal, *Le Réalisme*).[85] But his own aims in *Madame Bovary* involved the rendering with great imaginative fidelity and no small amount of historical and other research of a certain world, that of provincial Normandy thirty years before, all of which he would have known perfectly well amounted to realism of a sort, which is to say that we are not entitled to assume that he would not have been interested in Courbet simply on the basis of the latter's profession of pictorial faith. (The critic Sainte-Beuve's first of three articles on *Salammbô*, written in 1862, makes it clear that on the strength of *Madame Bovary* Flaubert had come to stand for novelistic realism.[86])

And in fact even a cursory glance at an illustration of the *Burial* reveals how much it has in common with Flaubert's description: the cortège itself (Courbet subtly emphasizes its serpentine movement, echoing the river landscape), the coffin-bearers (six in *Madame Bovary*, four in the *Burial*), the priests, the two choirboys, the elevated cross, the women in black mantles, the candles (in the painting held by the choirboys), the cloth with tears covering the coffin (a black cloth with white tears in the novel, the reverse in the painting), the open grave with reddish earth piled at its verge, the *goupillon* or aspergillum (in the painting, still in its stoup of holy water – in *Courbet's Realism* I interpret it as a surrogate for the painter's brush), the country setting (different, of course, in the two cases) . . . To be sure, nothing in all this points unequivocally to Flaubert's awareness of the painting; his description of Emma's funeral procession and burial might equally have been based simply on his knowledge of actual funerals in and around Rouen. But I find it difficult to believe that he would not have recognized in Emma's funeral an opportunity at once to subsume and to go beyond the *Burial* (beyond its "mere" realism, it may be). At any rate, that is one way of understanding the emphasis throughout the quoted passage on various sounds and, to a lesser degree, on odors: the prayers of the priests, cantors, and choirboys, the creaking of a distant carriage, the cry of a cock and the thudding of a horse's hooves, the smell of burning wax, the *silent* sliding of loosened earth into the open grave (a brilliant touch), and then the onomatopoetic "choc" of the coffin as it reached the bottom of the grave, the grating noise of the cords with which it had been lowered being retracted, and finally, climactically, the clatter of the first shovelfuls of earth against the wooden coffin, a climax further marked by the wholly unexpected "nous" (the first word in the novel, it will be remembered) and its even more surprising present-tense verb, breaking with the two past tenses governing the rest of the passage ("ce bruit formidable qui nous semble être le retentissement de l'éternité").

Such effects inevitably lie beyond the ordinary evocative capacities of the art of painting, despite Courbet's lifelong interest in evocations of sound (though there is also a sense in which the sudden "nous" and the use of the present tense create a distancing effect not unlike that between the beholder and the painted scene). But so does, on wholly different grounds, the intensely visual sentence, a capsule masterpiece of Flaubertian prose, "Une brise fraîche soufflait, les seigles et les colzas verdoyaient, des gouttelettes de rosée tremblaient au bord du chemin, sur les haies d'épines." By this I mean, in the first place, that no painting could hope to match the notation of *extremely slight* movement cumulatively conveyed by the verbs "soufflait," "verdoyaient," and "tremblaient"; and in the second, that there is – as elsewhere in the novel – something intensely visual as well in the actual play of the verbal signifiers, down to the level of individual phonemes or indeed letters (the z in "colzas" snags my attention every time I read that sentence; it is itself a kind of thorn, preparing the reader for the "épines" to come). As I have tried to show, this sort of linguistic micro-activity is one of the hallmarks of Flaubert's prose in *Madame Bovary*, though the present instance has a rather different flavor from the other examples of it we have considered. My point in this coda is simply to suggest that an awareness, however mediated, of Courbet's early and in many respects supreme display of pictorial strength may have prompted a special effort of writing on Flaubert's part when it became time to bury Emma Bovary.[87]

One last remark: Courbet's Pavillon du Réalisme, competing with the official display of French and foreign painting in the nearby Exposition Universelle, opened to the public on 28 June 1855.[88] On 27 June, Flaubert in Croisset closed a letter to his friend Louis Bouilhet by saying that he felt the need not to think about his novel for the next fifteen days. It seems he was about to go to Paris. "I'm going to give myself over to painting, to the Beaux-Arts. *That sets up a man.*" In his idiomatic French: "Je me livrerai à la peinture, aux Beaux-arts, *cela pose un homme*" (585; emphasis in original).[89]

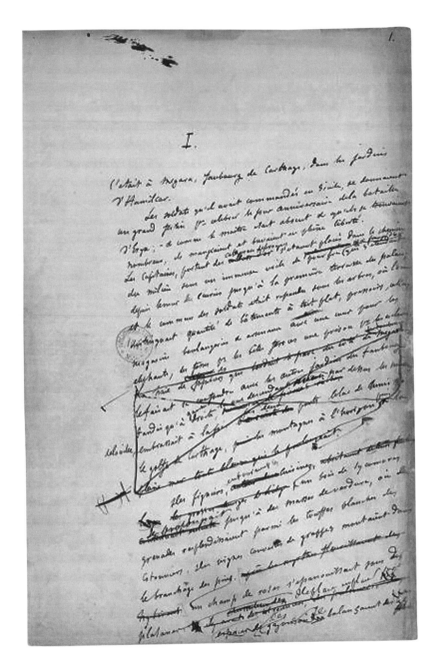

Gustave Flaubert, manuscript of *Salammbô*. Collection of the Bibliothèque nationale de France, Département des manuscrits, MS NAF 23656, folio 1r.

WILLING *SALAMMBÔ*

Books aren't made like children but like pyramids, with a
premeditated design and by carrying one great block on top
of another, and it takes guts, time, and sweat, and it isn't good
for anything! and it stays in the desert! albeit prodigiously
dominating it. The jackals piss on the base and the bourgeois
climb up it – continue the comparison.
> – Gustave Flaubert to Ernest Feydeau[1]

Finally, my permanent advice is this: *will!*
> – Gustave Flaubert to Mlle Leroyer de Chantepie[2]

1

Shortly after finishing *Madame Bovary*, even before it appeared in book
form, Flaubert turned to a new project: revising *La Tentation de saint
Antoine*, the original manuscript of which, on the advice of his friends
Louis Bouilhet and Maxime Du Camp, he had reluctantly set aside in
1849. (Not long after that painful episode he and Du Camp traveled
together to the Middle East, a sojurn of eighteen months. Within a few
months of returning to Croisset, he began to plan and then to write
Madame Bovary.) In fact Théophile Gautier published excerpts from the
revised portions of *La Tentation* in the journal *L'Artiste* in late 1856 and
early 1857. Soon, however, Flaubert realized that the time had not come
to deal with the entire manuscript and turned instead to a wholly new
project – a novel set in ancient Carthage immediately following the conclusion of the first Punic War against Rome, at the time of the so-called
"war of the mercenaries" (240–238 BCE) in which the large mercenary
army enlisted by Carthage in its struggle with Rome turned against its
former employer on the grounds that the latter had reneged on promises

of payment. The war itself, as reported by the ancient historian Polybius, was famously savage; it ended with the destruction of the mercenary army at the hands of the Carthaginian general Hamilcar, father of the more famous Hannibal, but it also involved a prolonged siege of Carthage, battles in which the losses on both sides were great, and numerous incidents of such depraved cruelty as to give that war legendary status in the world of antiquity.

Salammbô took roughly five years to compose, including almost two months in 1858 when Flaubert visited the site of ancient Carthage and its environs in order to gather first-hand information about the physical setting and architectural remains. On his return he jettisoned what he had written to date, or at least seriously revised it in the light of his experience on the ground. Throughout his campaign on the novel Flaubert read extensively in ancient texts, scholarly treatises on Carthage and North Africa, publications of all sorts on ancient myths and religions. All this could not make him proof against pedantic and ill-willed scholarly attack once the book was published, but it enabled him to give at least as good as he got when he replied to his chief detractor, a German named Guillaume Froehner.[3]

As the *Correspondance* attests, the actual writing of *Salammbô* was a long ordeal. Not that literary composition was ever a simple matter for Flaubert. But various letters to Ernest Feydeau and Edmond and Jules de Goncourt, among others, testify to a sense of extreme difficulty, hardly surprising in light of the extraordinary nature of his undertaking. To Feydeau in late November, 1857: "What a bitch of a subject! I'm switching back and forth between the most extravagant emphasis and the most academic platitude. Turn by turn, it feels like Pétrus Borel or Jacques Delille [i.e., an arch-romantic and a translator from the classics]. Word of honor! I'm afraid it might be devilishly banal and rococo. On the other hand, since it must be *violent*, I fall into melodrama. Good grief, it's to break your head against." And: "The difficulty lies in finding the *right* note. That is achieved by an excessive *condensation* of the idea, be it naturally or by willpower, but it's not easy to imagine a constant truth, that is, a series of details salient and probable in a world two thousand years distant. Also, to be understood, there needs to be a kind of permanent translation, and what an abyss this opens up between the absolute and the work."[4] To Mlle Leroyer de Chantepie (23 January 1858): "The book I'm now writing will be so distant from modern customs that – since there is no resemblance possible between my heroes and readers – it will find little interest. There will be no observations, nothing of what is generally liked. It will be Art, pure Art, and nothing else. I don't know of a more difficult task. Fellow writers who know my intentions are frightened by the attempt. I might be showered with ridicule for the rest of my life."[5] (He goes on to say that he absolutely must make a voyage to the site.) To Feydeau (mid-October 1858): "Ever since literature came to exist, no has tried to do anything this crazy. It's a work bristling with difficulties: to give people a language *in which they have not thought!*"[6] To Feydeau (19 December 1858): "Seriously, I believe *never* has anyone undertaken so difficult a subject from the point of view of style. At every line, at every word, language fails me and the insufficiency of vocabulary is such that I am very often forced to change the details. I'll croak, my old friend, I'll croak. Never mind, it's beginning to amuse me devilishly."[7] To Théophile Gautier (27 January 1859): "I don't know what will become of my *Salammbô*. It's extremely difficult. I'm breaking my back. But I guarantee, oh Master, that my intentions are virtuous. It's not an idea, that proves nothing at all. Instead of speaking, my characters *roar* [or *bellow* or *howl*; the French is *"hurlent"*]. From end to end, it's the color of blood. There are men's brothels, cannibalism, elephants, and torture. But it might well be that all this is profoundly stupid and perfectly boring. When will it be done? God knows."[8] To Mlle Leroyer de Chantepie (18 February 1859): "I have besides taken on an unrealizable thing."[9] To Feydeau (29 November 1859): "One must be absolutely mad to take on books of this sort. At each line, at each word, I overcome difficulties no one will appreciate, and perhaps they will be right not to. For if my system is false, the work is a failure."[10] To Feydeau again (21 October 1860): "It seems to me that all my sentences are cut the same way and that that is fatally boring. My will meanwhile does not weaken, and as content that becomes pretty."[11] And again (15 July 1861): "*Carthage* is going to make me burst with rage. I'm full of doubts now, about the whole, the general plan; I think there are too many troops? That's the history, I know. But if a novel is as annoying as a scholarly book, good night, there's no more art. . . . My will, however, doesn't weaken at all, and I go on."[12] To Jules Duplan (25 September 1861): "I am physically exhausted. My muscles ache. Bovary's poisoning made me puke into my chamber pot. The assault on Carthage makes my arms sore. – And yet that is the most pleasant thing this job has to offer! – and then the thought of all the inanities I'll provoke people to say about my book depresses me in advance. When I was in the thick of it, this perspective cheered me up. Right now, it appals me."[13] And to the Goncourts near the end (2 January 1862): "I am about halfway through my last chapter. I'm giving in to farces that will provoke disgust in good society. I'm piling horrors upon horrors. 20,000 of my guys have just starved to death and eaten one another: the rest will end up under the feet of elephants and beween the jaws of lions."[14]

As for the story itself, I am going to assume that there is no need to summarize the plot beyond saying that the chief characters are Salammbô, daughter of the Carthaginian Hamilcar Barca and a priestess in the cult of Tanit, a Carthaginian deity; Hamilcar himself, an immensely rich and supremely competent man who at a crucial juncture is appointed (in fact reappointed) leader of the Carthaginian forces; Hannon, another leading Carthaginian and political rival of Hamilcar's, who suffers from a hideous leprosy-like disease that in the course of the novel renders him ever more disfigured; the Lybian Mâtho, a mercenary leader of tremendous stature and prowess who becomes obsessed with Salammbô and her beauty when he first lays eyes on her in the novel's opening scene; the Numidian prince Narr'Havas, a rival for Salammbô and eventually an open supporter of the Carthaginian cause (in return for which Hamilcar promises him Salammbô in marriage); and Spendius, a Greek former slave, who emerges as a major inciter of the war, close companion of Mâtho, and an indefatigable opponent of Carthage until his eventual capture and crucifixion. Also important are three "objects": a sacred textile, "le zaïmph," which covers the statue of Tanit in the latter's temple in Carthage ("the 'zaïmph'" is captured by Mâtho and Spendius early in the war and then is retaken by Salammbô in the novel's crucial scene, in which she is sexually possessed by Mâtho in his tent); a fine gold "chaînette" that runs between Salammbô's ankles, attesting to her virginity, until it is broken during the encounter in the tent; and the giant iron figure of the bull-headed masculine god Moloch, in which the children of leading Carthaginians are burned alive in order to bring an end to a drought threatening the city's survival (the mercenaries having disrupted the normal flow of water to the city via an aqueduct). A sacred snake, a python, is Salammbô's companion until it dies following the recovery of the "zaïmph," leaving her, we are told, indifferent. In the penultimate chapter the mercenary army is brilliantly maneuvered by Hamilcar into a sort of enclosed valley among rocks, the "défilé de la Hache" ["defile of the axe"], where they are starved to death and their remains are eaten by lions; Spendius is crucified; and Mâtho, brought back to Carthage, is handed over to the populace to be torn apart. The novel ends with his death, indeed with the extraction of his heart, immediately followed by the death of Salammbô. The last sentence reads: "Ainsi mourut la fille d'Hamilcar pour avoir touché au manteau de Tanit."[15] ["Thus died Hamilcar's daughter, for touching Tanit's veil."][16]

Not surprisingly, *Salammbô* itself was and remains, as Jacques Neefs puts it in his preface to the recent Livre de Poche edition, "of a resisting strangeness" (7). My purpose in this essay is not at all to diminish that sense of strangeness or indeed of resistance but rather to try to account for both by offering a reading of the novel that will take as immediate context the analysis just put forward of the interplay of style and habit, intention and automatism, in *Madame Bovary*. In fact it was when I read *Salammbô* immediately after finishing a draft of my essay on *Madame Bovary* that I realized that I had no choice but to write the present essay.

2

Here are the opening four paragraphs of *Salammbô*:

> C'était à Mégara, faubourg de Carthage, dans les jardins de Hamilcar.
>
> Les soldats qu'ils avait commandés en Sicile [i.e., the army of mercenaries] se donne un grand festin pour célébrer le jour anniversaire de la bataille d'Éryx, et, comme le maître était absent et qu'ils se trouvaient nombreux, ils mangeait et ils buvaient en pleine liberté.
>
> Les capitaines, portant des cothurnes de bronze, s'étaient placés dans le chemin du milieu, sous un voile de pourpre à franges d'or, qui s'étendait depuis le mur des écuries jusqu'à la première terrasse du palais; le commun des soldats était répandu sous les arbres, où l'on distinguait quantité de bâtiments à toit plat, pressoirs, celliers, magasins, boulangeries et arsenaux, avec une cour pour les éléphants, des fosses pour les bêtes féroces, une prison pour les esclaves.
>
> Des figuiers entouraient les cuisines; un bois de sycomores se prolongeait jusqu'à des masses de verdure, où des grenades resplendissaient parmi les touffes blanches des cotonniers; des vignes, chargées de grappes, montaient dans le branchage des pins; un champ de roses s'épanouissait sous des platanes; de place en place sur des gazons, se balançaient des lis; un sable noir, mêlé à de la poudre de corail, parsemait les sentiers; et, au milieu, l'avenue des cyprès faisait d'un bout à l'autre comme une double colonnade d'obélisques verts. (43–4)

> It was at Megara, a suburb of Carthage, in Hamilcar's gardens.
>
> The soldiers whom he had commanded in Sicily were treating themselves to a great feast to celebrate the anniversary of the battle of Eryx, and as their master was away and there were a large number of them, they ate and drank in complete freedom.
>
> The captains, in their bronze buskins, had occupied the central path, under a purple, gold-fringed awning, which stretched from the stable wall to the first terrace of the palace; the bulk of the soldiers were spread out under the trees, where numerous flat-roofed buildings could be seen, presses, cellars, stores, bakeries, and arsenals, with a yard for the elephants, pits for the wild beasts, a prison for the slaves.

Fig-trees surrounded the kitchens; a sycamore wood extended as far as clumps of greenery, where pomegranates shone resplendent among the white tufts of the cotton-shrubs; vines, heavy with bunches of fruit, climbed up the pine branches; a bed of roses bloomed beneath the plane-trees; here and there on the lawns lilies swayed; the paths were sprinkled with black sand, mixed with powdered coral, and in the middle the cypress avenue stretched from one end to the other with a double colonnade of green obelisks. (17)

To take them in order: the first paragraph consists in a single sentence, one that has become somewhat famous among readers of the novel. "C'était à Mégara –" Immediately the reader is faced with a foreign name, which however is immediately explained – "faubourg de Carthage" – and then served up with a second, "Hamilcar," which is not. The laconic formulation "C'était" – "it was" – will recur countless times in the pages that follow, as critics have not failed to notice.[17] What I have not seen remarked, however, is that throughout the novel the imperfect tense carries none of the implications of repetitive or characteristic actions – "he would walk" rather than "he walked," for example – that often marks Flaubert's use of it in *Madame Bovary*. (Often in conjunction with the present participle in the same sentence, as Proust was the first to note.)[18] In other words, the opening sentence alone starts *Salammbô* on a very different path stylistically speaking from that pursued in *Madame Bovary*.

The second paragraph conveys further information, namely that Hamilcar commanded soldiers in Sicily (during the first Punic War, which understandably is never named as such) and that the scene in question takes place on the anniversary of the Battle of Eryx, an event that is unlikely to have prompted the memory of many readers.

Two paragraphs, two sentences. The third paragraph, too, comprises a single sentence, one that early on deploys the word "cothurnes," defined by Neefs in a footnote in the latest edition of the novel as "in Greece and Rome, shoes that went halfway up the leg" (43). (He adds: *Bronze* here is a mark of nobility and war" [43].) Not that the word itself would have been wholly unfamiliar to educated Frenchmen in Flaubert's time: it appears in a range of nineteenth-century texts by Chateaubriand, Charles

Nodier, Hugo, Gautier, Gérard de Nerval, Théodore de Banville, Leconte de Lisle, and Flaubert himself (e.g., in the 1849 *Tentation*).[19] But it was not a common noun, and in any case it is the gradual unfolding of the single sentence that seems especially noteworthy, not simply because of its remarkable construction (I am resisting the impulse to analyze that in detail) but also, even more important, though in a sense inseparable from the issue of its construction, because of the extent to which the very progress of the sentence in the act of reading (and rereading: this is not a sentence to be read just once and left behind) involves a heightened recognition of a virtual counterpoint of effects of alliteration and repetition of the sort tracked in passage after passage in *Madame Bovary* earlier in this book. In fact the comparison with *Madame Bovary* is somewhat misleading: there is perhaps no single sentence in the earlier novel that matches the sheer deliberateness, the extreme compositional complexity, palpably at work in this one.

Move on to paragraph four, another, even longer though in other respects ultimately simpler single sentence, and the structure of repetitions – hard *g*'s, *t*'s, *c*'s, *p*'s, *b*'s, *v*'s, for a start – all but leaps to the eye (I mean it is no longer simply a matter of "aural" effects: even the punctuation, the repeated semi-colons, takes part in it). And here too, even more strongly than in paragraph three if that is possible, one has the sense (at any rate, I have the sense) of absolute authorial control, the impression, put more strongly the conviction, that all the alliterations and consonances and repetitions, and beyond that the complex phonic/visual phonemic pattern to which they give rise, have been intended as such by the writer. This is to say that paragraph four, like the three others we have looked at though perhaps most perspicuously of them all, appears devoid of the least hint of automatism of any kind.

Flaubert's contemporary, the vastly accomplished and influential critic Charles-Augustin Sainte-Beuve who wrote three long articles largely critical of *Salammbô*, seems to have had a partial intuition of what is going on. (I shall be making heavy use of Sainte-Beuve's articles in what follows; basically they are full of pertinent observations, almost all of which are turned against Flaubert, which is to say that the critic has only the most fitful and deflected insights into the novelist's project. But his testimony is invaluable.) On several occasions in his series of articles, Sainte-Beuve singles out individual paragraphs as aesthetically satisfying in themselves, as for example in the following passage from the second article. "Read the following paragraph out loud," he writes, "scanning it like poetic prose, and you'll be struck by the tone and the number [i.e., the handling of syllables]":

> Souvent, au milieu du jour, le soleil perdait ses rayons tout à coup. Alors, le golfe et la pleine mer semblaient immobiles comme du plomb fondu. Un nuage de poussière brune, perpendiculairement étalé, accourait en tourbillonnant; les palmiers se courbaient, le ciel disparaissait, on entendait rebondir des pierres sur la croupe des animaux; et le Gaulois, les lèvres collées contre les trous de sa tente, râlait d'épuisement et de mélancolie. Il songeait à la senteur des pâturages par les matins d'automne, à des flocons de neige, aux beuglements des aurochs perdus dans le brouillard; et, fermant ses paupières, il croyait apercevoir les feux des longues cabanes, couvertes de paille, trembler sur les marais, au fond des bois. (162)[20]

> Often, in the middle of the day, the sun suddenly lost its radiance. Then the gulf and the open sea looked as still as molten lead. A cloud of brown dust, stretching straight up, swirled rapidly upward; the palm trees bent, the sky disappeared, stones could be heard bouncing off the backs of animals; and the Gaul, lips stuck to the hole of his tent, moaned with exhaustion and gloom. He thought of how the meadows smelled on autumn mornings, of snowflakes, of how the aurochs lowed when they were lost in the mist, and closing his eyes, he imagined he could see the fires of the long, straw-roofed huts, flickering over the marshes, in the depth of the woods. (94)

For all its brevity, the paragraph is – even by the standards of *Madame Bovary* – exceptionally dense with phonemic repetition, and once again the impression of deliberate construction is unmistakable. Also suggestive from my point of view is Sainte-Beuve's recommendation that the passage be read "out loud," or as he says slightly further on in relation to another passage, "in a loud voice" (217). The latter passage, less obviously charged with repetitions but nevertheless a tour de force of internal echoes and accords, goes:

> Les Grecs, avec la pointe de leurs glaives, creusèrent des fosses. Les Spartiates, retirant leurs manteaux rouges, en enveloppèrent les morts; les Athéniens les étendaient la face vers le soleil levant; les Cantabres les enfouissaient sous un monceau de cailloux; les Nasamons les pliaient en deux avec des courroies de boeufs, et les Garamantes allèrent les ensevelir sur la plage, afin qu'ils fussent perpétuellement arrosés par les flots. Mais les Latins se désolaient de ne pas recueillir leurs cendres dans les urnes; les Nomades regrettaient la chaleur des sables où les corps se momifient, et les Celtes, trois pierres brutes – sous un ciel pluvieux, au fond d'un golfe plein d'îlots. (309)

> The Greeks dug pits with their sword points. The Spartans took off their red cloaks and wrapped them round the dead; the Athenians laid them out facing the rising sun; the Cantabrians buried them beneath a heap of stones; the Nasamones bent them in two with oxhide straps, and the Garamantes went to inter them on the beach so that they should be for ever watered by the waves. But the Latins were grieved not to be able to collect the ashes in urns; the Nomads missed the hot sands in which bodies become mummified, and the Celts missed the three rough stones, beneath a rainy sky, deep in a bay full of islands. (197)

Now, Sainte-Beuve in 1862 knew Flaubert socially (also Flaubert's literary friends the Goncourts) and would certainly have been aware of the writer's autograph practice of the "gueuloir." In effect, then, Sainte-Beuve was proposing that the reader virtually mime the vocal operations that had gone into the making and testing of the paragraphs in question – as if the very practice of the "gueuloir" was imagined by him as actively evoked by the prose of *Salammbô* as never quite by that of *Madame Bovary*.

This brings me to my basic claim about Flaubert's project in *Salammbô*: I understand that novel as the product of a sustained attempt to produce a work of literature which not only on the stylistic level (though that remains primary) but in every other respect that the writer could control would be exclusively the product of conscious intention, of the faculty of will – "volonté" – and which therefore would appear devoid of the effects of habit or automatism of the sort that I have tried to show are continually at work in the prose of *Madame Bovary*.*

3

Consider for example Flaubert's highly controversial decision to set the novel in ancient Carthage at the time of the war of the mercenaries. Such a decision meant not only that the novel would deal with unfamiliar events but also that the war itself was one that bore no connection with the subsequent flow of European history owing to the total destruction of Carthage by Rome in the second Punic War. This is the point of one of Sainte-Beuve's pertinent but in the end obtuse criticisms of the novel: How could Flaubert have expected readers to care about this "lost war,

---

* I am deliberately not amassing further examples of such paragraphs as evidence for this claim, though some will inevitably come to the fore in the course of this essay. Here, however, is a list of twenty such paragraphs, short and long, drawn from different parts of *Salammbô*, each of which to my mind fits the characterization in terms of effects of will in the absence of effects of automatism that I have just proposed for the passages cited above. The paragraphs are listed by page number or numbers and also by the opening phrase: 64–5, "Mais une barre lumineuse . . ."; 77, "La route s'allongeait . . ."; 97–8, "La lune se levait . . ."; 133, "Cette première enceinte . . ."; 163, "En face de lui . . ."; 182, "La ville descendait . . ."; 199, "Leurs coureurs et leurs cochers . . ."; 211, "Abdalonim, en pâlissant . . ."; 240–41, "Par-dessus la voix . . ."; 262, "Cependant, les vivres . . ."; 284–5, "Personne n'apparaissait . . ."; 286, "Aux clarets du crepuscule . . ."; 302, "Les longues files . . ."; 307, "On reconnaissait la forme . . ."; 326, "La confusion des armes . . ."; 355, "La terrasse était maintenant . . ."; 374, "Elle tomba toute la nuit . . ."; 375, "On avait exposé . . ."; 397, "Enfin ils s'arrêtent . . ."; 423–4, "Des chevilles aux hanches . . .". Needless to say, the number twenty is arbitrary; I could have listed many more such paragraphs.

buried in the defiles or the sands of Africa," he asks rhetorically. "What is the duel between Tunis and Carthage to me? Talk to me about the duel between Carthage and Rome, fine, I'm all attentive and engaged. In the intractable quarrel between Rome and Carthage, all future civilization is already at stake; our own civilization depends on it; our own, whose torch was lit at the Capitol's altar, just as that of Roman civilization was lit at the burning of Corinth" (225). In contrast, Flaubert's subject seemed to him "strange, remote, savage, bristling, almost inaccessible" (199), forfeiting from the start all "human sympathy" for his characters and their interactions.

This, however, was precisely the point of Flaubert's choice of subject, as the critic Albert Thibaudet recognized in his 1935 monograph on the author. Thibaudet writes:

> If he has chosen this Carthaginian subject so very deliberately, it is because communications between Carthage and us are pretty much cut off, because Carthage figures in classical antiquity as an isolated block, an aerolite foreign by virtue of its civilization to its surroundings, a kind of singular city that has, it seems, disappeared without leaving behind anything whatsoever in the common current of culture. In this way, Flaubert takes a subject that is a stranger to the human continuity of the West, just as in *Madame Bovary* he thought of taking a subject that was a stranger to its inner current, a subject that stands by itself, purified from all attachment to the here and now, a subject that can be treated uniquely from the point of view of style.[21]

The allusion to *Madame Bovary* is to the point just so long as one does not fail to acknowledge the magnitude of the difference between the two subjects – between a domestic tragedy in provincial France during the July Monarchy and an epic confrontation set in the remote past between a distinctly alien civilization that subsequently was wiped from the face of the globe and a polyglot army that is itself totally annihilated by the end of the later novel. Put slightly differently, as Sainte-Beuve remarks, the great success of *Madame Bovary*, not to mention Flaubert's victory in court when the government brought suit against the novel for obscenity, made literary realism the watchword of the day as far as fiction was concerned (198); what was now wanted from the author was a second novel some-what in the vein of *Madame Bovary* but extending realism's reach, at once a pendant and a contrast (as Sainte-Beuve puts it), moving beyond the restricted canvas of the earlier novel to engage more broadly with con-temporary life (something on the order of *L'Education sentimentale*, one might think). Surely Flaubert would have been aware of this expectation on the part of his admirers, which of course makes his decision to write *Salammbô*, a novel in which the idea of realism as currently understood had absolutely no purchase, all the more striking. As Thibaudet suggests, the subject of *Salammbô* was designed so that Flaubert could treat it "uniquely from the point of view of style"; my further suggestion is that the style in question was one designed to foreground the action of autho-rial will at every point.[22]

4

The constant resort to unfamiliar proper names, place-names, and names of objects plays a role in this as well; the proper nouns "Megara," "Hamil-car," and "Eryx" as well as the common noun "cothurnes," all from the first three paragraphs in the novel, are minor instances of this, as are the designations "Cantabres," "Nasamons," and "Garamantes" in the second paragraph quoted by Sainte-Beuve. A more typical passage reads:

> Les Carthaginois se trouvaient encore dans l'effroi de leur arrivée [of the barbarians gathered to lay siege to the city], quand ils aperçurent, venant droit vers eux, comme des monstres et comme des édifices, – avec leurs mâts, leurs bras, leurs cordages, leurs articula-tions, leurs chapiteaux et leurs carapaces, – les machines de siège qu'envoyaient les villes tyriennes: soixante carrobalistes, quatre-vingts onagres, trente scorpions, cinquante tollénones, douze béliers et trois gigantesques catapultes qui lançaient des morceaux de roche du poids de quinze talents. (327)

The Carthaginians were still horror-stricken by their arrival when they saw, coming straight towards them, what looked like monsters and buildings, with their masts, arms, rigging, joints, roofs, and carapaces, the siege engines sent by the Tyrian towns: sixty carrobalistae, eighty onagers, thirty scorpions, fifty swing beams, twelve rams, and three gigantic catapults which hurled boulders weighing fifteen talents. (209)

Or this, further on in the siege: "Les trois grandes catapultes ne s'arrê-taient pas. Leurs ravages étaient extraordinaire; ainsi, la tête d'un homme alla rebondir sur le fronton des Syssites; dans la rue de Kinisdo, une femme qui accouchait fut écrasée par un bloc de marbre, et son enfant avec le lit emporté jusqu'au Carrefour de Cinasyn, où l'on retrouva la couverture" (346). ["The three great catapults, despite all these labours, did not stop. The damage they did was extraordinary; thus, a man's head bounced up against the pediment of the Syssitia; in Kinisdo street a woman in labour was crushed by a marble slab and her child with the bed carried as far as the Cinasyn crossroads, where the blanket was found" (222–3).] Earlier Hamilcar's chief of fleets replies to a question from the former, "qu'il avait envoyé une flotte par Gadès et Thymiamata, pour tâcher d'attein-dre Eziongaber, en doublant la Corne-du-sud et le promontoire des Aro-mates" (205). ["He answered that he had sent a fleet by Gades and Thymiamata to try and reach Eziongabar, rounding the Southern Horn and the Spice promontory" (124).] Still earlier, Salammbô calls the names of the sacred fish wantonly killed by the mercenaries, names that are also those of months: "Siv! Sivan! Tammouz, Eloul, Tischri, Schebar!" (58) And after the final defeat of the mercenaries, a garden in Carthage is described as follows: "Les colombes, sur les palmiers autour d'eux, roucoulaient doucement, et d'autres oiseaux voletaient parmi les herbes: des galéoles à collier, des cailles de Tartessus et des pintades puniques. Le jardin, depuis longtemps inculte, avait multiplié ses verdures; des colo-quintes montaient dans le branchage des canéficiers, des asclépias parse-maient les champs de roses, toutes sortes de végétations formaient des entrelacements, des berceaux . . ." (399). ["The doves on the palm-trees around them softly cooed, and other birds fluttered among the plants: ringed galeoli, Tartessus quails, and Punic guinea-fowl. The garden, long neglected, had grown profusely; colocynths climbed up into the branches of cassias, asclepiads dotted the rose beds, all kinds of vegetation had entwined and formed arbours . . ." (260)] But perhaps the most bravura passage of this sort is found in the long chapter in which Hamilcar visits the underground chambers that contain his immense wealth, however diminished the latter is by the losses of war and the depredations of the mercenaries. One chamber in particular contains innumerable jewels:

> Avec son flambeau, il alluma une lampe de mineur fixée au bonnet de l'idole; des feux verts, jaunes, bleus, violets, couleur de vin, couleur de sang, tout à coup illuminèrent la salle. Elle était pleine de pierreries qui se trouvaient dans des calebasses d'or accrochées comme des lampadaires aux lames d'airan, ou dans leurs blocs natifs rangés au bas du mur. C'étaient des callaïs arrachées des montagnes à coups de fronde, des escarboucles formées par l'urine des lynx, des glossopètres tombés de la lune, des tyanos, des diamants, des sandastrum, des béryls, avec les trois espèces de rubis, les quatre espèces de saphir et les douze espèces d'émeraudes. Elles fulguraient, pareilles à des éclaboussures de lait, à des glaçons bleus, à de la poussière d'argent, et jetaient leurs lumières en nappes, en rayons, en étoiles. Les céraunies engendrées par le tonerre étincelaient près des calcédoines qui guérissent les poisons. Il y avait des topazes du mont Zabarca pour prévenir les terreurs, des opals de la Bactriane qui empêchent les avortements, et des cornes d'Ammon que l'on place sous les lits afin d'avoir des songes. (214–15)

> He used his torch to light a miner's lamp fixed to the idol's cap; the room was suddenly lit up with a blaze of green, yellow, blue, violet, purple, crimson fires. It was full of precious stones contained in gold calabashes hooked like lamps on to bronze sheets, or in their original blocks arranged along the bottom of the wall. There were callais torn from the mountains by slingshots, carbuncles formed by lynx's urine, glossopetri fallen from the moon, tyanos, diamonds, sandastrum, beryls, the three kinds of rubies, four kinds of sapphire, and twelve kinds of emeralds. They flashed, like splashes of milk, blue icicles, silver dust, and shed their light in sheets, rays, stars. Ceraunites engen-

dered by thunder twinkled near chalcedonies, which are a cure for poisons. There were topazes from Mount Zabarca to ward off terrors, opals from Bactria which prevent miscarriages, and horns of Ammon which can be put under the bed to inspire dreams. (129)

And so on, to a greater or lesser degree, throughout the book. All of which led Sainte-Beuve to complain that Flaubert had failed to provide an "indispensable instrument," namely a map of Carthage along with a plan of the isthmus, of other relevant locales, and of major monuments such as he conceived them, adding that it would also be helpful to have "a glossary at the end of the book, in which the strange words we encounter for the first time would be precisely defined and explained" (211).

Nothing, however, except perhaps his publisher's proposal that the book appear with illustrations,[23] could have run more counter to Flaubert's project, which (whatever else it involved) was precisely to confront the reader with the sheer willfulness of the writing, its insistence from first to last upon determining its own terms of intelligibility without regard for the reader's prior knowledge or habitual assumptions. In his carefully crafted response to Sainte-Beuve, Flaubert claimed that in effect he defined all the foreign words as he went along,[24] but of course that isn't true; if the reader doesn't know what a "céraunie" or a "calcédoine" is, or for that matter where to find "le promontoire des Aromates," he or she is out of luck – hence the annotations in modern editions of the novel, of which Flaubert surely would have disapproved. (As for the twelve kinds of emeralds, what could any modern editor hope to do by way of enumerating them?[25])

One further, small but telling point is relevant here: the peculiar, wholly original orthography that Flaubert chose for the names of three of his principal characters: Salammbô (why the two *m*'s and the circumflex over the *o*?), Mâtho (again, why the circumflex?), and Narr'Havas (which Flaubert spells as "Naravasse" in his reply to Froehner, offering no serious justification for the change of orthography in the novel[26]). "You will have been able to guess that the two *m*'s in Salammbô are used on purpose to pronounce Salam and not Salan," Flaubert remarks to Froehner (who had criticized him on those grounds), which makes a sort of limited sense but says nothing about the circumflex over the *o*; "Mâtho," with its circumflex over the *a*, goes unmentioned. My suggestion is that the strange orthography of the three names – also, of course, that of the invented name "zaïmph"[27] – expresses nothing so much as a certain authorial will, as if each time one or the other of the names recurs, as they continually do, the reader is in effect meant to be reminded of the writer's free and in a sense perfectly arbitrary decision to notate those names in just this way and not another.

5

Then there is the undeniable fact that the leading characters, Hamilcar, Salammbô, Mâtho, and the others, are almost wholly devoid of psychological traits that would make them even passably "real" to the reader. Only Spendius, perhaps, in his mixture of intrepidness, resentment, intelligence, and impulsiveness, could manage the transition into another, more standard sort of novel. The others are abstract and at times grandiose; it is hardly surprising that Sainte-Beuve found something operatic about Mâtho's raid on the "zaïmph" (213) or that Gautier actually tried to commission an opera from Verdi on the subject (the project fell through).[28] Once again Sainte-Beuve stresses the impossibility of feeling sympathy for Flaubert's heroes; Mâtho's hopeless passion for Salammbô seems to him false and artificial, while Salammbô herself strikes him as a reworking of Chateaubriand's Atala. Sainte-Beuve further notes that in the course of the long chapter narrating Hamilcar's visit to the subterranean chambers of his house that hold the various stores of his riches, "the author's aim is not to show Hamilcar's character, he only wants to show the stores" (214). (This is largely true, though we are also given instances of Hamilcar's casual brutality.) Needless to say, Flaubert was aware of the problem, as the remarks to various correspondents cited previously clearly state. Indeed the deliberate denial of sympathy and attachment for the leading characters is thrown into sharp relief by two short passages involving elephants: the first when Hamilcar after visiting his stores is approached by one of his three surviving beasts who has had his trunk cut off and who attempts to caress him "avec l'extrémité hideuse de son moignon" (224) ["with the end of its hideous stump" (135)], drawing tears from Hamilcar, a unique event; and the second when, in the course of the long and brutal battle of Macar, "un éléphant monstrueux qu'on appelait *Fureur de Baal*, pris par la jambe entre des chaînes, resta jusqu'au soir à hurler, avec une flèche dans l'oeil" (242) ["a monstrous elephant known as 'Baal's Wrath,' caught by the leg between the chains, stayed bellowing until evening with an arrow in its eye" (148)] – perhaps the most unforgettable image in the entire novel.

What has not been recognized, however, is that the psychological "unreality" of the leading characters goes hand in hand with a consistent thematization of the issue of will and its opposite, automatism. Most explicitly, Salammbô and Mâtho are depicted throughout the novel as in the grip of virtual hypnosis in relation to each other. This emerges in the opening scene in Hamilcar's garden when Salammbô suddenly appears on the uppermost terrace of the family palace, descends flights of stairs to lament the family's sacred fish murdered by the mercenaries, then approaches the latter and stands for several minutes with her eyes closed "à savourer l'agitation de tous ces hommes" (62) ["savouring the excitement of all these men" (28)] – "mimetically" opening herself to the violent emotion around her.[29] At this point Mâtho, who from the moment of her apparition has looked on spellbound, leans toward her, whereupon the text reads: "Involontairement elle s'en approcha, et, poussée par la reconnaissance de son orgueil, elle lui versa dans une coupe d'or un long jet de vin, pour se réconcilier avec l'armée" (62) ["Involuntarily she drew nearer to him, and moved to acknowledge his pride she poured him a long stream of wine into a golden cup to reconcile herself with the army" (28)].[30] This has immediate consequences we need not go into; what is crucial is the adverb with which the sentence begins, all the more so in that it recurs at two further, strategic junctures: once as Salammbô embarks on her mission to recover the "zaïmph" from Mâtho (285) and again, decisively, at the end of the novel as Mâtho, being torn apart by vengeful Carthaginians, meets Salammbô's gaze. "Dès le premier pas qu'il avait fait," we read, "elle s'était levée; puis involontairement, à mesure qu'il se rapprochait, elle s'était avancée peu à peu jusqu'au bord de la terrasse; et bientôt, toutes les choses extérieures s'effaçant, elle n'avait aperçu que Mâtho. Un silence s'était fait dans son âme, – un de ces abîmes où le monde entier disparaît sous la pression d'une pensée unique, d'un souvenir, d'un regard. Cet homme, qui marchait vers elle, l'attirait" (428–9). ["From the first step he took she had stood up; then, involuntarily, as he drew nearer, she had gradually come further forward to the edge of the terrace; and soon all the outside world was blotted out and she saw only Mâtho. Her soul was filled with silence, one of those abysses in which the whole world disappears beneath the pressure of a single thought, memory, look. This man walking towards her attracted her to him" (281).] (The depth of Salammbô's somnambulism is such that she seems never to realize fully what took place in the tent or indeed that her feelings for Mâtho are what can only be called sexual.) Mâtho, for his part, is from the first all but unmanned by his hopeless passion for her, which sexually possessing her in the tent does nothing to abate. One early moment is especially significant with respect to the issues I am tracing. On the road to Sicca, Mâtho complains to Spendius that Salammbô obsesses him and bitterly weeps in frustration; to which Spendius replies, "'Sois fort, mon maître! Appelle ta volonté et n'implore plus les Dieux . . .'" (83–4) ["Be strong, master! Summon up your will and stop imploring the Gods . . ." (42)]. In other words, both Salammbô and Mâtho are presented to the reader under the sign of their powerful involuntary – and in Salammbô's case, largely unrecognized – mutual attraction; this is the entire principle of Mâtho's actions throughout the war, to Spendius's frustration. (Mâtho does have his moments, however. Before the battle of Macar "une volonté superbe fulgurait dans ses yeux, pareille à la flamme d'un sacrifice" [230] ["an arrogant will flashed in his eyes, like the flame of a sacrifice" (139)].)

As for Hamilcar, he is, I want to say, a titan of "volonté," though in fact Flaubert never refers to him in those terms. Rather, one has to infer as much from his actions throughout the novel, in particular from his military leadership, which even in the worst days of the siege is unflagging

("tout pliait sous la violence de son génie" [228] ["all bent before the violence of his spirit" (138)], we are told of his reform of the Carthaginian
army before the battle of Macar), as well as from his tactical brilliance,
which in the end, after months of maneuvering, induces the mercenary
army to enter the deadly trap of the "défilé de la Hache." "Jamais son
génie ne fut aussi impétueux et fertile" (379) ["His genius had never been
so impetuous and fertile" (246)], Flaubert writes just before the trap is
sprung. There is, however, one atypical incident that seems designed to
bring out the extent to which Hamilcar's will was placed under strain in
an especially tender regard. At one point during his nighttime interview
with the Elders, when he was still refusing their insistence that he take
charge of the Punic forces, he is told that the mercenary who made off
with the "zaïmph" – Mâtho – was seen leaving his daughter's chamber,
presumably after having had intercourse with her (which was not yet the
case). Hamilcar's response is unexpected: he tears off his tiara, literally
mounts the altar of Moloch, and proceeds to swear an elaborate oath:

> "Par les cent flambeaux de vos Intelligences! par les huit feux des
> Kabyres! par les étoiles, les météores et les volcans! par tout ce qui
> brûle! par la soif du Désert et la salure de l'Océan! par la caverne
> d'Hadrumète et l'empire des Ames! par l'extermination! par la cendre
> de vos fils, et la cendre des frères de vos aïeux, avec qui maintenant je
> confonds la mienne! Vous, les Cent du Conseil de Carthage, vous avez
> menti en accusant ma fille! Et moi, Hamilcar Barca, Suffète-de-la-mer,
> Chef des Riches et Dominateur du peuple, devant Moloch-à-tête-de-
> taureau, je jure: . . ." On s'attendait à quelque chose d'épouvantable; il
> reprit d'une voix plus haute et plus calme: "Que même je ne lui en par-
> lerai pas!" (198)

> "By the hundred torches of your Intelligences! By the eight fires of
> the Cabiri! By the stars, meteors, and volcanoes! By all that burns! by
> the thirst of the Desert and the salt of the Ocean! By the cave of
> Hadrumetum and the kingdom of the Spirits! By slaughter! By the
> ashes of your sons and the ashes of your ancestors' brothers, with
> which I now mingle my own! You, the hundred members of the

Council of Carthage, you lied when you accused my daughter! And I, Hamilcar Barca, Suffete of the sea, Chief of the Rich and Dominator of the people, before bullheaded Moloch I swear . . ." They waited for something dreadful, but he went on in a louder and calmer voice: "That I will not even mention it to her!" (119)

And throughout the remainder of the novel, even after Salammbô returns from her encounter with Mâtho in his tent with the "zaïmph" in her possession and with the gold ankle "chaînette" broken, Hamilcar keeps his word. More precisely, he asks repeatedly about what took place between Mâtho and her, but never confronts her with the accusation that she had given up her virginity. I understand the oath scene, with its quasi-parodistic Balzacian intensity, as one designed to foreground the issue of will in connection with Hamilcar. (Baudelaire, in his 1859 article on Théophile Gautier, says of Balzac's characters, "All the souls are weapons loaded to the muzzle with will" ["Toutes les âmes sont des armes chargées de volonté jusqu'à la gueule"].[31] "Loaded with will" precisely characterizes Hamilcar, never more palpably so than in this scene. Speaking of "gueules," Hamilcar's face is referred to in paragraph five of chapter one as "solennel et impénétrable" [44] ["solemn and impenetrable" (17)] – just what one would expect of a figure such as he.) If we then take seriously the fact that both Salammbô and Mâtho are expunged at the novel's end, the possibility arises that the narrative interplay among Hamilcar, Salammbô, and Mâtho is to be read as allegorizing the triumph of will over automatism. But even if one hesitates to go that far, it is fascinating, and obviously significant, that will and automatism – two basic terms for the preceding analysis of Flaubert's prose in *Madame Bovary* – have been portioned out in *Salammbô* in that mutually exclusive manner.*

---

*   An extreme distinction – in that sense a separation – between will and automatism is at work, I have tried to show, in Courbet's *The Quarry* (*La Curée*) of 1856–7 (Fig. 11), the last of what I think of as his allegories of Realism. See Michael Fried, *Courbet's Realism* (Chicago and London, 1990), pp. 180–82. But in the first place the hunter, or hunter–painter, is portrayed as in a largely passive condition (his very hands are tucked out of sight), while the suggestion of will and effort has been displaced onto the *piqueur*

11　Gustave Courbet, *The Quarry*, oil on canvas, 1856–7. Boston, Museum of Fine Arts.

6

Commentators have always been struck, and almost without exception disconcerted, by the prevalence in *Salammbô* of protracted and extraordinarily detailed descriptions of various sorts. Three examples from the opening chapters are in no way unusual. First, our initial sighting, if that is the word, of Salammbô herself:

> Sa chevelure, poudrée d'un sable violet, et réunie en forme de tour selon la mode des vierges chananéennes, la faisait paraître plus grande. Des tresses de perles attachées à ses tempes descendaient jusqu'aux coins de sa bouche, rose comme une grenade entrouverte. Il y avait sur sa poitrine un assemblage de pierres lumineuses, imitant par leur bigarrure les écailles d'une murène. Ses bras, garnis de diamants, sortaient nus de sa tunique sans manches, étoilée de fleurs rouges sur un fond tout noir. Elle portait entre les chevilles une chaînette d'or pour régler sa marche, et son grand manteau de pourpre sombre, taillé dans une étoffe inconnue, traînait derrière elle, faisant à chacun de ses pas comme une large vague qui la suivait. (57)

> Her hair, powdered with mauve sand, was piled up like a tower in the style of the Canaanite virgins and made her look taller. Ropes of pearls fastened to her temples fell to the corners of her mouth, rose red like a half-open pomegranate. On her breast clustered luminous stones iridescent as a lamprey's scales. Her arms, adorned with diamonds, were left bare outside a sleeveless tunic, spangled with red flowers on a dead black background. Between her ankles she wore a golden chain to control her pace, and her great, dark purple mantle, cut from some unknown material, trailed a broad wake behind her with every step she took. (25)

---

blowing his hunting horn; and in the second my account of the painting emphasizes the notion of continuity between the two extremes, which is not at all the point of my remarks about *Salammbô*. In fact it is immediately following my discussion of *The Quarry* that I first introduce the topic of Ravaisson's *De l'habitude*.

(Another tour de force of phonemic construction, by the way.) Then there is this account of the rearmost portion of the mercenary army and its followers on the road to Sicca:

> Puis vint la cohue des bagages, des bêtes de somme et des traînards. Des malades gémissaient sur des dromadaires; d'autres s'appuyaient, en boitant, sur le tronçon d'une pique. Les ivrognes emportaient des outres, les voraces des quartiers de viande, des gâteaux, des fruits, du beurre dans des feuilles de figuier, de la neige dans des sacs de toile. On en voyait avec des parasols à la main, avec des perroquets sur l'épaule. Ils se faisaient suivre par des dogues, par des gazelles ou des panthères. Des femmes de race libyque, montées sur des ânes, invectivaient les négresses qui avaient abandonné pour les soldats des lupanars de Malqua [one of the three quarters of Carthage]; plusieurs allaitaient des enfants suspendus à leur poitrine dans une lanière de cuir. Les mulets, que l'on aiguillonnait avec la pointe des glaives, pliaient l'échine sous le fardeau des tentes; et il y avait une quantité de valets et de porteurs d'eau, hâves, jaunis par les fièvres et tout sales de vermine, écume de la plèbe carthaginoise, qui s'attachait aux Barbares. (72)

> Then came the throng of the baggage train, the animals, and stragglers. The sick groaned on dromedaries; others limped along, supported on the stump of a pike. Drunkards carried off wineskins, those greedy for food took hunks of meat, cakes, fruit, butter wrapped in fig leaves, snow in linen bags. Some appeared holding parasols, with parrots on their shoulders. They had mastiffs, gazelles, or panthers following them. Libyan women, riding on donkeys, reviled Negresses who had abandoned the brothels of Malqua for the soldiers; a number of them suckled children slung round their necks on a leather strap. The mules, spurred on at sword point, bent double under the load of the tents; and there were many servants and water-carriers, wan and yellow with fever, filthy and verminous, scum of the Carthaginian populace, who joined the Barbarians. (34)

(That, too.) And finally a portion of the description of Carthage as viewed by the mercenaries following their return from Sicca:

La colline de l'Acropole, au centre de Byrsa [another quarter of the city], disparaissait sous un désordre de monuments. C'étaient des temples à colonnes torses avec des chapiteaux de bronze et des chaînes de métal, des cônes en pierres sèches à bandes d'azur, des coupoles de cuivre, des architraves de marbre, des contreforts babyloniens, des obélisques posant sur leur pointe comme des flambeaux renversés. Les péristyles atteignaient aux frontons; les volutes se déroulaient entre les colonnades; des murailles de granit supportaient des cloisons de tuile; tout cela montait l'un sur l'autre en se cachant à demi, d'une façon merveilleuse et incompréhensibe. On y sentait la succession des âges et comme des souvenirs de patries oubliées. (110)

The Acropolis hill, in the centre of Byrsa, was covered over with a litter of monuments. There were temples with twisted pillars, bronze capitals, and metal chains, cones of dry stone with azure stripes, copper cupolas, marble architraves, Babylonian buttresses, obelisks balancing on their points like upturned torches. Peristyles reached to pediments; scrolls unfolded between colonnades; granite walls supported tile partitions; in all this one thing was piled on another, half-hiding it, in a marvelous and unintelligible way. There was a feeling of successive ages and, as it were, memories of forgotten lands. (59)

(Also that.)

As the second citation in particular shows, there is throughout *Salammbô* no firm distinction to be made between description and narration; here as elsewhere narration proceeds largely by description, though one might also say, in view of the novel's apparent stake in the latter, that narration of a sort often provides an occasion and in a sense a justification for description, which of course was Gotthold Ephraim Lessing's view of Homer's inspired narrative of the making of Achilles's shield. This is especially true of the long central chapter entitled "Hamilcar Barca," in the course of which Hamilcar, returned to Carthage, first attends a secret nighttime meeting with the city Elders in the depths of the Temple of Moloch and then, in his own house, surveys his diminished but still substantial wealth (as we saw, Sainte-Beuve was disturbed precisely by Flaubert's emphasis in the latter episode on the wealth rather than on Hamilcar's character). The passage cited previously full of names of jewels comes from that episode.

Discomfort with the extremely prominent role played by description in *Salammbô* begins early. "There is great exhaustion in these never-ending descriptions, in this button-by-button indication of characters, in this miniature depiction of each costume," Edmond and Jules de Goncourt wrote in their *Journal* after Flaubert read to them chapters one through eleven in a single sitting. "The greatness of the armies thereby disappears. The effects become petty and concentrated on a single point; clothing tramples over faces, landscapes over feelings."[32] (No one could have less sympathy for the Goncourts than I, but imagine having to sit through a reading of two-thirds of the novel, even by Flaubert.) This is also a major theme in Sainte-Beuve, who on the one hand is impressed by individual passages, especially those describing landscapes, but on the other objects both to the sheer quantity of description and to the unwavering intensity of the prose. "Since descriptions make up the bulk of the book," he writes in his third article, "I have to say a few words about them. What there is of landscape description is marked by exactitude, by relief, sometimes by African grandeur, but, all in all, by a lot of monotony. I would like more gradation, and that natural perspective be observed. I will never get used to this picturesque procedure that consists in describing to the point of satiation, and with almost equal perspicuousness, that which we do not see and cannot reasonably notice" (227) – blue stones underfoot at night, for example. Indeed the arduousness of the entire project, the sense of sheer writerly effort that pervades every page, seems to him deeply problematic. "The author does not hold himself above his work; he engages too much, he has his nose against it; he seems not to have considered it in its entirety either before or after, nor to master it at any moment. He has never stepped back from his work sufficiently to adopt the point of view of his readers" (224). In consequence, everything is "forced, sought after, belabored, researched, dug up, much stranger and weirder than it is original" (224) (bringing us back, in a different spirit, to Jacques Neefs's "resisting strangeness"). As Sainte-Beuve also remarks, "All the pain that was involved in writing it, he passes on to us" (224) – a rather brilliant statement, perhaps the most acute in the three articles.

One other set of remarks by Sainte-Beuve goes further in bringing his qualms about description in *Salammbô* into intellectual focus. "Put strongly," he writes as if addressing Flaubert, "if all you describe to me were true, copied from nature, I would be interested in a different sense, not because it would be art but because it would be a positive document, as one is interested in the reports of a traveler, an authentic account of Japanese customs. But you invent, you conjecture, and as soon as you do that, you lose me" (225). This may seem a bit simple-minded (a few pages later, Sainte-Beuve goes on to suggest that Flaubert should really have written a travel book about the ruins of Carthage!), but in fact it corresponds to something readers of *Salammbô* have always felt, namely, the almost incommensurable disproportion between what would have been or indeed is today knowable about ancient Carthage and more broadly the war of the mercenaries and the relentless and minutely detailed technical, architectural, and sensuous precision of Flaubert's descriptions. It is as if the term "description" itself doesn't quite seem appropriate here, and in fact Gautier in his highly laudatory article on the novel describes the departure of the mercenaries for Sicca, one paragraph of which has just been quoted, as not a description but "an evocation,"[33] a word, however, that fails to capture the sense of sheer invention – of naked assertion – one feels is continually in play. (As if the writer were relentlessly creating, or re-creating, the world he is ostensibly describing. And as if the reader were intended to feel that this is what is going on.) The Hamilcar-surveying-his-jewels paragraph is a magnificently hyperbolic case in point, though one short passage from earlier in the same chapter made an even stronger impression of this sort when I first encountered it. Hamilcar is about to meet secretly with one hundred Elders to discuss the desperate straits in which Carthage has found itself. There are also four "pontiffs" presiding over the occasion; these are described as follows: "Les quatre pontifes se tenaient au milieu, dos à dos, sur quatre sièges d'ivoire formant la croix: le grand-prêtre d'Eschmoûn en robe d'hyacinthe, le grand-prêtre de Tanit en robe de lin blanc, le grand-prêtre de Khamon en robe de laine fauve, et le grand-prêtre de Moloch en robe de pourpre" (188–9) ["The four pontiffs stayed in the middle, back to back, on four ivory seats arranged in a cross, the high priest of Eschmoûn in a hyacinth robe, the high priest of Tanit in a white linen robe, the high priest of Khamon in a fawn woolen robe, the high priest of Moloch in one of purple" (112)]. As Sainte-Beuve remarks apropos of another passage, how could Flaubert possibly have known (in this case) about the four different robes the "pontiffs" were wearing, or for that matter the exact configuration in which they were sitting? Of course, this makes no sense whatever as an objection to a work of fiction. But that the thought nevertheless occurs to one – that the sentence itself seems deliberately to provoke it – is precisely the point.[34]

My view of this should by now be clear: I understand Flaubert's insistence throughout *Salammbô* on what I have called a hyperbolic mode of description – also the dual impression of monotony and also of immobility that has always been felt to go with it[35] – as a crucial component of his larger project of asserting by every means possible his writerly will or "volonté." Put slightly differently, it is as if the prose of *Salammbô* deliberately keeps a measured *distance* from the reader, even as the scenes, persons, and objects described by that prose vary dramatically in that regard (some are viewed from far away, others at extremely close range). That may be why Flaubert's "tableaux" were criticized by the Goncourts on the grounds that "all the planes are on the same plane" (194) and why Sainte-Beuve complained that in Flaubert's descriptions "each object comes to thrust into the foreground and to attract the gaze" (198) – in other words, whatever the ostensible distance from an implied observer of a particular scene, person, or object, the descriptions themselves are felt to confront the reader in the same, equally salient way. (Sainte-Beuve also noted what seemed to him a failure of "natural perspective.") It is true that the implication of the Goncourts' and Sainte-Beuve's remarks is that what I am calling distance seemed to them a kind of unvarying and monotonous nearness, as if everything being described occupied the same foreground, but of course nearness as such implies a certain distance (comparable to the distance from the reader of the words on the page) as against the virtual eclipse of distance that takes place when a reader is completely immersed in a text, thereby losing awareness, in a certain sense, of the words themselves.[36] (That we lack an agreed-upon phenomenology of reading means that my formulations are necessarily somewhat vague but I take it the point comes through.)

All this is nowhere more palpable, I think, than in the novel's many descriptions of crowds and armies, starting as early as the opening chapter in Hamilcar's garden. The most spectacular of such scenes, however, takes place in the fourth chapter, "Sous les murs de Carthage," when the mercenaries have returned to restate their demands on pain of war and Carthaginian citizens in large numbers visit the mercenary camp in the hope of pacifying them by one means or another:

> Le camp ressemblait à une ville, tant il était rempli de monde et d'agitation. Les deux foules distinctes se mêlait sans se confondre, l'une habillée de toile ou de laine avec des bonnets de feutre pareils à des pommes de pin, l'autre vêtue de fer et portant des casques. Au milieu des valets et des vendeurs ambulants circulaient des femmes de toutes nations, brunes comme des dattes mûres, verdâtres comme des olives, jaunes comme des oranges, vendues par des matelots, choisies dans les bouges, volées à des caravanes, prises dans le sac de villes, que l'on fatiguait d'amour tant qu'elles étaient jeunes, qu'on accablait de coups lorsqu'elles étaient vieilles, et qui mouraient dans les déroutes au bord des chemins, parmi les bagages, avec les bêtes de somme abandonnées. Les épouses des Nomades balançaient sur leurs talons des robes en poil de dromadaire, carrées, et de couleurs fauve; des musiciennes de la Cyrénaïque, envelopées de gazes violettes et les sourcils peints, chantaient accroupies sur des nattes; de vieilles Négresses aux mamelles pendantes ramassaient, pour faire du feu, des fientes d'animal que l'on desséchait au soleil; les Syracusaines avaient des plaques d'or dans la chevelure, les femmes des Lusitaniens des colliers de coquillages, les Gauloises des peaux de loup sur leur poitrine blanche; et des enfants robustes, couverts de vermine, nus, incirconcis, donnaient aux passants des coups dans le ventre avec leur tête, ou venaient par-derrière, comme de jeunes tigres, les mordre aux mains. (115–16)

The camp looked like a town, it was so full of people and movement. The two distinct crowds mingled without becoming confused,
the one dressed in linen or wool with felt caps like pine cones, and the
other dressed in armour and helmeted. In the midst of the servants and
pedlars women of every nation circulated, brown as ripe dates, sallow
as olives, yellow as oranges, sold by sailors, chosen from hovels, stolen
from caravans, taken at the capture of towns, worn out by love-making
while they were young, constantly beaten when they were old, dying
by the roadside in retreats, among the baggage, with the abandoned
pack animals. The Nomads' wives swayed in their square, dun-coloured
dresses of dromedary hair; musicians from Cyrenaica, swathed in
violet gauze and with painted eyebrows, sang squatting on rush mats;
old Negresses with pendulous breasts picked up for fuel animal drop-
pings which they dried in the sun; Syracusan women had gold plates
in their hair, the Lusitanians seashell necklaces, the Gauls wolfskins on
their white breasts; and sturdy children, verminous, naked, uncircum-
scribed, butted passers-by in the stomach, or came up behind like tiger
cubs to bite their hands. (62–3)

Here is what *doesn't* happen when Flaubert in *Salammbô* depicts a crowd:
there is no imagination of merger, of being overwhelmed by sheer
numbers, of feeling one's identity slip away in the crush of total
anonymity. (The distinctness of the two crowds, one of Carthaginians,
the other of mercenaries, draws attention to this from the start.) In other
words, *Salammbô's* crowds are not at all like Poe's in "The Man of the
Crowd" or, even more to the point, Baudelaire's, who translated Poe's
story and during precisely the years when Flaubert was writing *Salammbô*
was thematizing the great urban crowd in poems, prose poems, and his
valedictory masterpiece of art criticism, "Le Peintre de la vie moderne."[37]
Rather, the mass of mercenaries is for Flaubert above all an occasion to
demonstrate his dumbfounding mastery of national and racial specifici-
ties as well as of the sadly typical life histories of the women who in this
paragraph claim the lion's share of his attention (the term of comparison
and contrast here would be with "Les Petites vieilles"). The sharp-focus
succession of sensuous and cultural particulars, culminating in the unex-

pected epithet "incirconcis," perfectly illustrates what the Goncourts and Sainte-Beuve found unnerving: from what consistent point of view could all these particulars have been seen and marshaled into a compelling whole? Answer: from no point of view other than that of the writer, pen in hand, looking down on his page. (I suspect that recognition of this simple fact on the part of modern commentators has been blunted by the experience of movies, in particular wide-screen ancient world epics with teeming crowd scenes; a paragraph like the above is routinely characterized as "cinematic," which on the one hand makes perfect sense but on the other, for the purposes of criticism, is too easy – we miss its true distinction.)

And indeed simply as prose, the paragraph in question is still another masterpiece of phonemic organization, perhaps the subtlest, most artfully measured, we have yet considered; again, what I want to stress is the absence of any hint that the alliterations and repetitions that emerge in close reading (the many *v*-words, for example, or the sequence "faire"– "feu"–"fientes") can possibly have escaped the writer's conscious notice. It would have been the chief work of the "gueuloir" in this and similar instances to weigh those alliterations and repetitions (and variations, and syncopations) judiciously before setting them definitively in place.

7

As Sainte-Beuve recognized – though in fact he says less about it than might have been expected – *Salammbô* revels in scene after scene of exceptional and explicit violence, cruelty, atrocity, hideousness. This indeed would seem to have been a major source of Flaubert's interest in the "inexpiable" war of the mercenaries (the adjective is Polybius's), that it offered countless opportunities for the literary depiction of such scenes in as much detail as could be wished. The brief description of the elephant *Fureur de Baal* bellowing with rage and pain because of the arrow in his eye is an almost incidental case in point, given the scale of the violence elsewhere in the book. More characteristic is the discovery early on in the novel by the mercenaries on the road to Sicca of a long file of crucified lions (much later the Gaul Autharite, on his own cross, will say of them, "C'étaient nos frères!" [406] ["'They were our brothers!'" (265)]); or Hannon's progressive disfigurement described in revolting detail and culminating in his being stripped prior to being crucified (therefore in the revelation of the full horror of his condition [404]); or the protracted feeding of the Carthaginian children to the iron oven of the statue of Moloch (371–3); or the appalling piecemeal flaying of Mâtho in the last pages ("c'était une longue forme complètement rouge" [424], with nothing recognizably human about him except his eyes) ("he was just a long shape, completely red from top to bottom" [281]). There is also the following account of the torture by the barbarians (i.e., the mercenaries) of a group of Carthaginian prisoners:

> On les rangea par terre, dans un endroit aplati. Des sentinelles firent un cercle autour d'eux; et on laissa les femmes entrer, par trente ou quarante successivement. Voulant profiter du peu de temps qu'on leur donnait, elles couraient de l'un à l'autre, incertaines, palpitantes; puis, inclinées sur ces pauvres corps, elles les frappaient à tour de bras comme des lavandières qui battent les linges; en hurlant le nom de leurs époux [killed by the Carthaginians in battle], elles les déchiraient sous leurs ongles; elles leur crevèrent les yeux avec les aiguilles de leurs chevelures. Les hommes y vinrent ensuite, et ils les suppliciaient, depuis les pieds, qu'ils coupaient aux chevilles, jusqu'au front, dont ils levaient des couronnes de peau pour se mettre sur la tête. Les Mangeurs-des-choses-immondes furent atroces dans leurs imaginations. Ils envenimaient les blessures en y versant de la poussière, du vinaigre, des éclats de poterie; d'autres attendaient derrière eux; le sang coulait, et ils se réjouissaient comme font les vendangeurs autour des cuves fumantes. (312)

> They ranged them on the ground in a level spot. Sentries stood all round, and the women were let in, thirty or forty in turn at a time. Wanting to make the most of the little time allowed them, the women ran from one to another, hesitating, palpitating; then, leaning over these poor bodies, they hit them with all their might like washerwomen

beating linen; screaming the names of their husbands, they tore at them with their nails; they gouged out their eyes with their hairpins. The men came next, and tortured them from the feet, which they cut off at the ankles, to the brow, from which they took circlets of skin to wear on their heads. The Unclean-Eaters thought up atrocious things. They infected the wounds by pouring on them dust, vinegar, shards of pottery; others waited behind them; blood was flowing and they were as joyful as the wine-harvesters behind the bubbling vats. (198–9)

And this, a moment in the siege of Carthage when the defenders suddenly show themselves and repulse the attackers:

Les créneaux s'ouvrirent, en vomissant, comme des gueules de dragon, des feux et de la fumée; le sable s'éparpillait, entrait par le joint des armures; le pétrole s'attachait aux vêtements; le plomb liquide sautillait sur les casques, faisait des trous dans les chairs; une pluie d'étincelles s'éclaboussait contre les visages, – et des orbites sans yeux semblaient pleurer des larmes grosses comme des amandes. Des hommes, tout jaune d'huile, brûlaient par la chevelure. Ils se mettaient à courir, enflammaient les autres. On les étouffait en leur jetant, de loin, sur la face, des manteaux trempés de sang. (337)

Then the battlements opened, spewing forth, like dragon's mouths, fire and smoke; sand was sprinkled everywhere, came through the joints of the armour; petroleum struck their clothes; molten lead spattered over helmets, made holes in flesh; a shower of sparks splashed over faces – and eyeless sockets seemed to weep tears as big as almonds. Men, yellow with oil, had their hair on fire. They began to run, set fire to others. The flames were stifled by bloodsoaked cloaks thrown over their faces from a distance. (215–16)

In a further battle scene the corpses of slain mercenaries are too tightly packed to fall down. "Quelques-uns, les deux tempes traversées par une javeline, balançaient leur tête comme des ours. Des bouches ouvertes pour crier restaient béantes; des mains s'envolaient coupées" (350) ["Some, their temples transfixed by a javelin, swayed their heads like bears. Mouths open to cry remained gaping; hands flew as they were lopped off" (225)].[38] But the pièce de résistance in this vein may well be the long and detailed account of the effects of famine on the mercenaries trapped in the "défilé de la Hache." Not that all forty thousand perish in that manner. Toward the end a number try to escape but are surrounded and defeated; two "syntagmes" (units of a few hundred men) attempt to surrender but are bound and stretched out on the ground, and the elephants are summoned. "Les poitrines craquaient comme des coffres que l'on brise," Flaubert writes; "chacun de leurs pas en écrasait deux; leurs gros pieds enfonçaient dans les corps avec un mouvement des hanches qui les faisait paraître boiter. Ils continuaient, et allèrent jusqu'au bout" (395). ["Their chests cracked like boxes being broken; each of the elephants' steps crushed two; their great feet sank into the bodies with a twist of the hips that made them look lame. They continued and went on to the end" (257).] A small group of survivors is forced to fight each other to the death like gladiators, and the survivors of *that* are killed treacherously. There follows a detailed account of the engagement with and brutal extermination of one more mercenary army. Finally, in the last pages of the chapter we return to the "défilé de la Hache" to find well-fed lions ranging among the partly eaten corpses. All this only partly conveys the extent to which the novel seems positively to seek out occasions for comparable scenes and effects.

The question, of course, is what one is to make of the "sadique" aspect of the novel.[39] For Sainte-Beuve it is a serious flaw, attributed by him to a desire on the part of the author to contravene the expectations of a bourgeois audience. But there is a further possibility, namely, that the scenes of gratuitous violence, cruelty, and horror that punctuate *Salammbô* from start to finish are means of exacerbating the reader's awareness of the actions and choices of the writer, which is also to say of the writer's determination to subject the reader to his will even to the extent of shocking or disgusting or otherwise disconcerting him or her with his words. Indeed, there is a small detail in the account of the siege of Carthage, either invented by Flaubert or discovered in some ancient text about another war, that is to say the least suggestive in this connection. "Ce qu'il y avait de plus irritant," the novel states, "c'était les balles de frondeurs [shot from the besiegers' catapults]. Elles tombaient sur les toits, dans les jardins et au milieu des cours, tandis que l'on mangeait attablé devant un maigre repas et le coeur gros de soupirs. Ces atroces projectiles portaient des lettres gravées qui s'imprimaient dans les chairs; – et, sur les cadavres, on lisait des injures, telles que *pourceau, chacal, vermine*, et parfois des plaisanteries: *attrape!* ou: *je l'ai bien mérité*" (346). ["The greatest annoyance came from the slingers' shot. It fell on the roofs, into gardens, while people were sitting down to a meagre meal with heavy hearts. These horrible missiles bore letters engraved on them which imprinted themselves on the victim's body; and on corpses insults could be read, like *swine, jackal, vermin*, and sometimes jokes: 'catch!' or 'I deserved it'" (223).] Does it go too far to find in this last sentence an only somewhat hyperbolic image of a relation of text to reader that Flaubert in the more sadistic passages in *Salammbô* aspired to make his own?

Apropos of the ideal of impersonality, to which he remained committed,[40] there is one other small touch in which Flaubert himself – Flaubert "personally" – might just be visible (and audible). I am thinking of the excruciatingly wounded *Fureur de Baal*, who "resta jusqu'au soir à hurler" – one of Flaubert's favorite verbs for what he did at the "gueuloir." (It is also a verb that occurs frequently throughout *Salammbô*.) If this seems unlikely, I would first of all recall the "muselé" bull at the "Comices" in *Madame Bovary*, in which I saw a figure for the writer (no ordinary "veau" is what I called him), and would also note that among the names of dead elephants listed at one point in *Salammbô* is, improbably, "l'Hirondelle" (407), "Swallow" – the name of the stagecoach that carried Emma to and from her assignations with Léon in the earlier novel.[41] The latter point proves nothing, of course, but it at least implies a degree of self-reference with respect to elephants that opens the door to further interpretation. And look: *Fureur de Baal/ Flaubert*; I leave the arrow in the eye to my readers' imaginations. Note, too, that the appalling Hannon, having taken command of the Carthaginian forces, is described in Flaubert-like terms as well: "Dans son palais, la nuit, comme il ne pouvait dormir, pour se préparer à la bataille, il hurlait, d'une voix terrible, des manoeuvres de guerre" (160). ["In his palace at night, as he could not sleep, in preparation for battle he shouted out combat commands in a terrible voice" (92–3).] Evidently the agony of writing *Salammbô* did not preclude the occasional stroke of macabre humor.[42]

8

I do not pretend that all this amounts to a comprehensive interpretation of *Salammbô*; for example, Jeanne Bem, Françoise Gaillard, and others have argued persuasively for a certain range of connections between Flaubert's portrayal of ancient Carthage and his thoroughly disabused understanding of Second Empire France.[43] And there has been important work done on the precise treatment of the myths of Tanit and Moloch in the novel and its relation to the larger narrative.[44] But I am convinced – it has been the aim of this essay to demonstrate – that no aspect of Flaubert's enterprise in *Salammbô* compares in importance to his ambition to achieve a wholly willed ("voulu") mode of writing, one therefore which would go "beyond" the revolutionary achievement of *Madame Bovary* precisely as regards the mixture or mutual interpenetration throughout the earlier novel of will and automatism, style and habit. (This did not prevent Sainte-Beuve, in a laudatory article on *Madame Bovary*, from characterizing it as "first and foremost a book, a book that is composed, thought out, where everything holds together, where nothing is left to the chance of the pen, and in which the author or, better, the artist has done, from start to finish, what he wanted to do" ["ce qu'il a voulu"].[45] By any reasonable standard, this is the simple truth.) Put slightly differently, it is as if having completed *Madame Bovary*, Flaubert himself had some sort of inkling that the domination of style, of sheerly artistic intentionality, in that quintessential work of literary art was less than absolute, and as if, after dallying for a moment with *La Tentation de saint Antoine*, he quickly embarked on an all but impossibly arduous new project every parameter of which was designed to promote the values of writerly "volonté" over any other range of considerations. (This is not to say, of course, that he fully achieved his aim; what would it mean to make such a claim?) One form this took, Jacques Neefs has suggested, is of a "visionary" intensity,[46] to which I would add that the intensity is often – not only in the scenes of warfare and torture – such as to suggest a never-quite-explicit aggressiveness toward the reader, whose task it is to "absorb" and so to speak to "process" Flaubert's sentences and paragraphs as one might find oneself compelled to absorb and deal with a sequence of blows. (Neefs speaks of that "visionary" intensity and of *Salammbô*'s prose generally as exacting from the reader "slowness, repeated readings, curiosity, and a particular form of assent" [33]; even as regards the most appalling and exhausting passages something of the last is still required. He also characterizes the prose of *Salammbô* as "willfully harassing" [34].[47]) This roughly is what I take Gautier to have meant when he refers to reading *Salammbô* as "one of the most violent intellectual sensations that one can experience" (254), even though he goes on to gloss the notion of violence mainly in terms of the quality of spectacle offered by that "strange, unknown world, overheated by the sun, motley with dazzling colors, glistening with jewels in the midst of a vertiginous atmosphere in which the emanations from perfumes mix with the vapors of blood" (254). The spectacle is indeed tremendous, but the "violent intellectual sensation" experienced by a reader brave enough to stay the course has to do with so much more.[48]

Some final points:

(1) It is striking that the early commentators on *Salammbô* often use the notion of "volonté" and its derivatives and synonyms in order to characterize Flaubert's project, but that they do so in a somewhat pejorative sense, the implication being that a certain willed effort is all too visible for the novel's good. "Let us respect the will of the artist," Sainte-Beuve writes early in the first article, "his fancy, and once we have exhaled our slight murmur [against the choice of subject; the murmur will swell in volume in the course of the articles], let us be led, docile, where it pleases him to lead us" (199) – a figure of speech that, without Sainte-Beuve recognizing the fact, tacitly and to my mind pertinently analogizes Flaubert to Hamilcar. (I refer by this to Hamilcar's tactical genius, leading on the mercenary army to its doom, but there is also a sense in which his

"solemn and impenetrable" face [44], mentioned at the end of the fifth paragraph of chapter one, is a compelling figure for the author's own ideal impassiveness.) Further on Sainte-Beuve refers to *Salammbô* as "this book of a laborious art" (203), and after introducing a comparison with Chateaubriand's *Les Martyrs*, he attributes to Flaubert "a more marked, more formal intention and pretention to restore everything about the past. Judging from the way in which he relies on each detail, each environing point, he seems not to have wanted to make a poem but rather a true, a real *tableau*" (203). And so on, culminating in the summary judgment, "Will has given him almost all his faults: may that same will take them from him" (231). In short, *Salammbô* was understood by Sainte-Beuve (and others[49]) as conspicuously and indeed excessively marked by authorial "volonté," but that in turn was not and has not subsequently been understood as the source and basis of a truly radical undertaking as well as of the novel's unique place in the history of modern, or should I say modernist, French literature.[50]

(2) There is, I want to claim, a larger context within which Flaubert's project in *Salammbô* can meaningfully be situated. In my book *Manet's Modernism, or, The Face of Painting in the 1860s*, I associated the work of artists of Manet's generation (Manet himself, Alphonse Legros, Henri Fantin-Latour, and James McNeill Whistler) with the writings of various critics (prominent among them Edmond Duranty) in which I detected what I characterized as a transvaluation of willing (of "le voulu") and related terms from a negative to a positive valence.[51] That is, epithets such as "willed" and "forced" had for generations carried a mainly negative evaluation, the implication being that the sense of effort they implied was too evident in the works that elicited those and related epithets from the critics of their time. Around 1860, however, the situation became transformed; as I put it in *Manet's Modernism*, "a new desire for pictorial intensity – more exactly, a desire for a new sort of pictorial intensity – changed the basic terms of problem by positively valorizing effects of forcing and willing within an absorptive framework" (194–5). A key painting in that connection was Legros's impressive *The Ex-Voto* (1860; Fig. 12) in Dijon, described by Duranty in an important essay as exhibiting "a forced

12   Alphonse Legros, *The Ex-Voto*, oil on canvas, 1860. Dijon, Musée des Beaux-Arts.

accord" between the character of the figures and "the very means of painting" (187). More broadly, I went on to associate the change with a radical acknowledgment of the beholder in advanced painting of that moment (195–7), epitomized by canvases such as Manet's *Old Musician* (1862; Fig. 13), *Déjeuner sur l'herbe* (1863), and *Olympia* (1863, exhibited 1865), which in turn amounted to a dialectical turning with respect to the issues of absorption and antitheatricality as they had been playing out in French painting starting in the 1750s if not earlier. (In *The Ex-Voto*, an absorptive picture, the acknowledgment can be felt in the turning of the panels of the ex-voto toward the viewer relative to the orientation of the post to which they are affixed.)

13   Edouard Manet, *The Old Musician*, oil on canvas, 1862. Washington, D.C., National Gallery of Art.

Let me quickly say that such a dialectic has no direct application to Flaubert or indeed to nineteenth-century French fiction generally. But might not the Flaubertian ideal of authorial impersonality, with its adamant and systematic denial of any suggestion of authorial address to the reader, be the equivalent of absorption in a certain sense of the term? Or even, in the case of *Salammbô*, of willing and forcing within an absorptive framework, the framework established by *Madame Bovary*? I leave both questions open. In any case, I suggest that there exists a strong analogy between the valorization of willing and forcing – also, I go on to propose, "facingness" and "strikingness" – in the pictorial discourse around Manet and his generation in the early 1860s and the many-faceted emphasis on the "voulu" that I have tried to show is central to Flaubert's undertaking in the exactly contemporary *Salammbô*. (Just how tricky and unstable issues concerning "volonté" were in the early 1860s can be seen in Flaubert's riposte to Sainte-Beuve's wish that he had included among his characters a "good" Greek, who would have contrasted morally with the figure of Spendius: "I have denied myself a contrast, that's true; but a facile contrast, a *willed* and false contrast."[52])

(3) Apropos the notion of strikingness, there is the violent incident in the chapter "Sous les murs de Carthage" in which the mercenaries, having drunk heavily, suddenly and for no reason decide to kill the Carthaginian slaves who had brought insufficient payment to them. "Ils devenaient terribles après le repas," the text reads, "quand ils avaient bu du vin! C'était une joie défendue sous peine de mort dans les armées puniques, et ils levaient leur coupe du côté de Carthage par dérision pour sa discipline. Puis ils revenaient vers les esclaves des finances et ils recommençaient à tuer. Le mot *frappe*, différent dans chaque langue, était compris de tous" (124). ["They became terrible after the meal, when they had drunk some wine! It was a joy forbidden on pain of death in the punic armies, and they raised their cup towards Carthage in derision at its discipline. Then they went back to the pay slaves and started killing again. The word 'strike!', different in each language, was understood by all" (68).] In fact the word "frappe" is taken from Michelet's account of the war in his *Histoire romaine* (Polybius relates a similar incident involving the phrase "Stone him"), but there is no mistaking Flaubert's relish in deploying it.

I should add that a major theme in the novel that has not yet been mentioned by me is the polyglot character of the barbarian armies, which has the cumulative effect of further distinguishing Flaubert's French (here epitomized by the word "frappe"). Early on in the novel there is also this: "Il y avait là des hommes de toutes les nations, des Ligures, des Lusitaniens, des Baléares, des Nègres et des fugitifs de Rome. On entendait, à côté du lourd patois dorien, retentir les syllabes celtiques bruissantes comme des chars de bataille, et les terminaisons ioniennes se heurtaient aux consonnes du désert, âpres comme des cris de chacal" (45). ["Men from every nation were there, Ligurians, Lusitanians, Balearics, Negroes, and fugitives from Rome. You could hear beside the heavy Doric dialect the Celtic syllables ringing out like battle chariots, and Ionian endings clashed with desert consonants, harsh as jackal-cries" (18).] This too has the effect of foregrounding Flaubert's French at the same time as it projects or say transposes onto the mercenary throng the intense play of syllables and phonemes threatening to undermine sense that was the hallmark of his own literary procedures.

The climax of the polyglot or aural "vacarme" theme comes just where one might expect it, in the climactic scene of Mâtho's martyrdom, where we are told: "Souvent une seule syllabe, – une intonation rauque, profonde, frénétique, – était répétée durant quelques minutes par le peuple entier. De la base au sommet les murs en vibraient, et les deux parois de la rue semblaient à Mâtho venir contre lui et l'enlever du sol, comme deux bras immenses qui l'étouffaient dans l'air" (427). ["Often a single syllable – a hoarse, deep, frenzied tone – was repeated for several minutes by the whole people. From top to bottom the walls shook with it, and the two sides of the street seemed to Mâtho to be coming at him and lifting him off the ground, like two huge arms choking him in the air" (280).] Whose arms are those, are we meant to imagine?

(4) The novel closes with a sentence that is by no means as simple as it looks: "Ainsi mourut la fille d'Hamilcar pour avoir touché au manteau de tanit" (430). ["Thus died Hamilcar's daughter, for touching Tanit's veil" (282).] As Veronica Forrest-Thomson was perhaps the first to observe, it is impossible for the reader to know what to make of this;[53] unlike any other sentence in the "voice" of the narrator, it embodies an appeal to a belief system that not only is not ours, it is one that has been systematically discredited in the course of the narrative. (For example, Hamilcar surreptitiously substitutes another man's son for his son Hannibal in the terrible scene of child sacrifice, but this blatant violation of the rite is soon followed not by any further punishment of Carthage but on the contrary by life-giving rains.) In Peter Starr's words, the sentence therefore "just sits on the page with the stupid *Dasein* of language" (53), a suggestive formulation which I would amend as follows: the sentence sits on the page as a piece of writing that no longer exactly belongs to the "world" of the novel, because the beliefs it ostensibly expresses have been invalidated by the novel itself, but also as one that does not quite come clear of that

"world" into the conceptual space "outside" it, where the claim is unintelligible and in effect leaves the reader staring in perplexity at the written or printed page. In other words, it is a sentence that must in effect be discarded or indeed cut, severed, in order for the novel at last to reach its end and for the reader to feel free to close the book and return definitively to his or her own world. Which is to say, in order for Flaubert to have fully realized the new, more exigent, at its most extreme deliberately rebarbative ideal of aesthetic autonomy that had governed the writing of *Salammbô* from the very first. I found myself thinking of that final sentence in these terms even before I came across the following in a letter from Flaubert to the Goncourts announcing the end of his travails: "I have finally resigned myself to considering as finished an interminable labor. Right now the umbilical cord is cut. Oof! Let's no longer think of it. It's a matter of going on to other exercises"[54] – as, with characteristic resolve, he proceeded to do.

(5) During the very years Flaubert wrestled with *Salammbô*, his greatest French literary contemporary, Charles Baudelaire, wrote the bulk of his so-called prose poems, the texts that constitute *Le Spleen de Paris*. No one, to my knowledge, has ever associated the prose poems with Flaubert's second major novel. But it is worth noting that writing to his mother from Brussels on 9 March 1865, Baudelaire explains that work on them has gone slowly both because of the depressing atmosphere of Brussels and because "having read the forty or fifty that have come out, you'll have guessed that the production of these little trifles is the result of a great concentration of the mind. Meanwhile, I hope I'll succeed in producing a singular work, more singular, *more willed at least*, than *Les Fleurs du mal*, in which I'll associate the frightful with the burlesque, and even tenderness with hatred."[55] The issue of "volonté," sometimes contrasted with terms such as "à son insu" ("without knowing it"), plays a major role in Baudelaire's art criticism, but there is hardly space to deal with that here.[56] My point is simply that one powerful motivation behind the prose poems may well have been the ambition to produce "poetic" texts every feature of which will have been determined by the intentions of the poet and not by the conventions of the sonnet or the rules governing the

alexandrine or the alternation of masculine and feminine rhymes, or even a certain idea of formal perfection inherent in the genre of lyric, and that this has an obvious parallel with my account of what Flaubert was up to in *Salammbô*. (The dedicatory pages to Arsène Houssaye end in the statement that the author "considers it the greatest honor of the poet to accomplish *just* what he set out to do."[57]) Not coincidentally, the prose poems also involve a new, more distanced and aggressive (more Manet-like?) relation to the reader than the *Fleurs du mal* poems, with the qualified exception of "Au lecteur."[58] This too is a topic for another occasion.[59]

(6) Nor is this the place to try to characterize the remainder of Flaubert's fictional oeuvre – *L'Éducation sentimentale*, *La Tentation de saint Antoine* (1875), *Trois Contes*, and *Bouvard et Pécuchet* – with respect to the issues of will and habit as they have been developed in this book. For what it is worth, my impression is that the grueling and prolonged effort that went into the writing of *Salammbô* had the effect of liberating Flaubert for the great project that followed, the composition of *L'Education sentimentale*, the prose of which – more dialogue-based than the previous two books – gives the impression of being happily free of the extraordinary stylistic (and no doubt psychic) burden under which its creator had labored for the previous five years. It may also be relevant that the last of Flaubert's literary projects, the writing of *Bouvard et Pécuchet*, which he died before completing, has as its twinned protagonists two professional copyists, who in the end will retreat from their earlier experiments in living to a practice of simple copying, just the filling of pages with writing, as they put it (in a plan for the second half of the book, which Flaubert did not live to write).[60] As if on the level of theme a writerly "volonté" reaches there a farthest limit to the exclusion of any other motivation. Obviously more could be said about Flaubert's oeuvre in the vein of the present study. But not by me – not at present, at any rate.

(7) It is worth adding just a word about Flaubert's correspondence with Mlle Leroyer de Chantepie, a middle-aged woman living just outside Angers who wrote him an intensely admiring letter after reading *Madame Bovary* in the *Revue de Paris* and with whom Flaubert went on to conduct a curious correspondence during the years of his labors on *Salammbô*. I

call the correspondence curious because it largely consists in long, unparagraphed, emotionally intense letters from Mlle Leroyer de Chantepie in which she complains bitterly about her life, her circumstances, her illnesses, her religious ambivalences, and so on, to which Flaubert most often responds by urging her to be less passive, to have the courage to change her circumstances, to come to Paris, to read more seriously, to take up "a *long* labor and promise to finish it" (30 March 1857).[61] Or again: "You need *forced* labor, something difficult and obligatory to do every day" (15 June 1859).[62] At one point he writes: "You ask how I cured myself of the nervous hallucinations to which I used to fall victim? (1) by studying them scientifically, that is to say, by setting out to account for them, and (2) by *the power of the will*" (18 May 1857).[63] Or, distilled down to a single sentence, "Finally, my permanent advice is this: *will!*" (11 July 1858).[64] My suggestion is that the exchange of letters with Mlle Leroyer de Chantepie provided Flaubert with an opportunity to "pass on the sting," as Elias Canetti puts it in *Crowds and Power*,[65] in effect urging her to follow his example as he goaded himself toward the completion of his nearly impossible task.

(8) One last point. The opposition between intention and automatism that I have identified as central both to *Madame Bovary* and to *Salammbô* will also mark the critical and theoretical discourse around art photography, starting in the late nineteenth century and continuing to the present day.[66] This opens intriguing perspectives – upon which I close.

NOTES

ABBREVIATIONS

Corr.: Gustave Flaubert, *Correspondance*, ed. Jean Bruneau, 5 vols. (Paris, 1973–2007).

Philippot: Didier Philippot, ed., *Gustave Flaubert. Mémoire de la critique* (Paris, 2006). [An invaluable compilation of critical texts on Flaubert from the 1850s to Thibaudet and Proust.]

STYLE AND HABIT IN *MADAME BOVARY*

1   Gustave Flaubert to Louise Colet, 24 April 1852, in *The Letters of Gustave Flaubert*, sel., ed., and trans. Francis Steegmuller (Cambridge, Mass., 1980), 1:158. For the original French see *Corr.*, 2:79.

2   Charles-Augustin Sainte-Beuve, "*Madame Bovary*, by Gustave Flaubert," in *Madame Bovary: Backgrounds and Sources, Essays in Criticism*, ed. Paul de Man (New York, 1965), 326. Translation slightly modified. For the original French see Sainte-Beuve, "*Madame Bovary*, par Gustave Flaubert," in Philippot, 139. Further page references to both de Man's and Philippot's respective compilations will be in parentheses in the text.

3   Edmond and Jules de Goncourt, entry for 10 December 1860, in *Paris and the Arts, 1851–1896: Pages from the Goncourt Journal*, ed. and trans. George J. Becker and Edith Philips (Ithaca, N.Y., 1971), 55. Further page references will be in parentheses in the text. For the original French see Edmond and Jules de Goncourt, *Journal. Mémoires de la vie littéraire*, ed. Robert Ricatte (1956; Paris, 1959), 1:642.

4   Charles Du Bos, "On the 'Inner Environment' in the Work of Flaubert," in de Man, *Madame Bovary*, 370. Further page references will be in parentheses in the text. For the original French see Du Bos, "Sur le milieu intérieur chez Flaubert" (originally published 1921), in *Approximations* (Paris, 2000), 170.

5   Roland Barthes, *S/Z: An Essay*, trans. Richard Miller (1970; New York, 1974), 140.

6   Guy de Maupassant, "Gustave Flaubert: A Study," in *The Complete Works of Gustave Flaubert: Embracing Romances, Travels, Comedies, Sketches and Correspondence* (London and New York, 1904), 3:xlvi. Translation modified. For the original French see Guy de Maupassant, "Gustave Flaubert [Extraits]," preface to *Lettres de Gustave Flaubert à*

George Sand (1884), in Philippot, 575. Further page references to both will be in parentheses in the text.

7   Ibid. Translation modified. For the original French see Philippot, 575.

8   "From the seclusion of a large family home on the banks of the Seine near Rouen, the so-called hermit of Croisset raises the art of prose narrative to new levels and reveals its modernity. As he stomps up and down the avenue of lime trees in his garden, sometimes in the company of his friend and mentor Louis Bouilhet, Flaubert bellows out the sentences of *Madame Bovary*, to the amazement or amusement of the folk in passing river craft. This is the legendary *gueuloir*, or 'yelling place', where the novelist puts his writing through the test of sound, rhythm and vocal fluidity, subjecting it to the final quality control." Timothy Unwin, "Gustave Flaubert, the hermit of Croisset," in *The Cambridge Companion to Flaubert*, ed. Timothy Unwin (Cambridge and New York, 2004), 1.

9   For the original French see Goncourt and Goncourt, *Journal*, 1:682.

10 For the original French see *Corr.*, 2:135.

11 For the original French see ibid., 139.

12 For the original French see ibid., 523.

13 Julian Barnes, "Writer's Writer and Writer's Writer's Writer," *London Review of Books*, 18 November 2010, 10. Indeed the terms of Flaubert's perfectionism remained constant throughout his career. Thus he wrote to George Sand almost a quarter-century later: "The concern for external Beauty you deplore in me is for me a *method*. When I come upon a disagreeable assonance or a repetition in one of my sentences, I'm sure I'm floundering in the False. By dint of searching, I find the proper expression, which was always the *only* one, and which is, at the same time, harmonious." Emphasis in original. 10 March 1876, in *Flaubert-Sand: The Correspondence*, trans. Francis Steegmuller and Barbara Bray (New York, 1993), 393. For the original French see *Corr.*, 5:26.

14 Gustave Flaubert, *Madame Bovary*, ed. Jacques Neefs (Paris, 1999), 58. Further page references will be in parentheses in the text.

15 Gustave Flaubert, *Madame Bovary*, trans. Francis Steegmuller (New York, 1957), 5–6. Further page references will be in parentheses in the text.

16 I have examined some, though by no means all, of the brouillons – manuscript drafts – for *Madame Bovary* that are in the collection of the Université de Rouen (available through the website http://flaubert.univ-rouen.fr) in an attempt to determine at what stage in the writing process the sorts of phonemic relationships that I have been stressing emerged in the text. My impression is that many of them were there from the first, but that in the course of subsequent drafts the density of relationships invariably thickened as the sentences in question assumed a kind of rhythmic inevitability. According to Pierre-Marc de Biasi, "the analysis of Flaubert's brouillons has brought

to light a large number of graphic markings that indicate the presence of an oral structuring of the writing, such that it can be traced and makes possible a reliable reconstruction of the textualization process that is the *gueuloir*: acoustic paradigms, units of breath, hunt for assonances, measuring the number of syllables, etc. – unpublished material that is of the highest interest to the new study of rhythm, of melody, of punctuation, too. The *gueuloir* is not a gimmick. . . . For Flaubert, during the most silent of readings we do of course read with our eyes but always also with our throat in that, at its prompting, we feel a genuine virtual music of words: the music that could become audible if we endowed with the least of breaths what is, in us, the infinitesimal but precise sketch of an articulation. Contemporary science seems very much to prove him right" ("LA VOIX: le gueuloir de Flaubert," *Le Magazine littéraire*, no. 401 [September 2001]: 39). The pioneering work exploiting the brouillons is Claudine Gothot-Mersch, *La Genèse de Madame Bovary* (Paris, 1966).

17 See, however, Vladimir Nabokov's attempt to draw Charles's "casquette" on one of the manuscript pages of his Cornell undergraduate course lecture about the book (*Lectures on Literature*, ed. Fredson Bowers [San Diego, New York, and London, 1982], 131).

18 Jean Ricardou, "Belligérance du texte," in *La Production du sens chez Flaubert*, Colloque de Cerisy, ed. Claudine Gothot-Mersch (Paris, 1975), 100. Emphasis in original. Further page references to this book will be in parentheses in the text.

19 Jonathan Culler, "The Uses of *Madame Bovary*," *Diacritics* 11, no. 3 (Autumn 1981): 78. A related phenomenon is noted by Jean-Pierre Richard in an essay on Flaubert's last novel, the unfinished *Bouvard et Pécuchet*. Bouvard is watching steers feeding in their shed at a barn. Richard cites the sentence, "Tous les boeufs avancèrent leurs mufles entre les barreaux et buvaient lentement." ["All the steers thrust their muzzles between the bars and drank slowly."] He continues:

> A beautiful sentence, so characteristic of Flaubert by virtue of the positioning of the long terminal adverb (the slowness there is at once signifier and signified), of the verbal dissemination of the imperfect and the simple past, by the bestial aspect too, gently bestial, connoting the satisfaction of desire. If the sentence succeeds in making the scene unanimous (*all* the steers), it nevertheless contains an obstacle, a sustained censure (*between the bars*). But there too the libidinal play of the letters transgresses in its way the the demi-barrier of the forms: the alliterative repetition of the labial *b* which goes from *bâtons* to *boeufs*, *barreaux*, *buvaient*, establishes a textural current of meaning, as homogeneous as that of the "petit filet d'eau" ["little stream of water"] which preceded, on the level of the signified, the coming [of the steers]. [The stream had appeared as if by a miracle.] In addition, the play of the letters has the advantage of referring directly to the name of the spectator fascinated by this scene, because it is really *Bouvard* who drinks ("boit") here, or

who drank ("buvait"), in and through these intercessor steers (critics have noted in his case, as with Charles *Bovary*, this bovine filiation). Behind Bouvard one will perhaps also hear [or understand] the name of the writer who fantasizes, in an animal mode – we know his profound taste for bestiality – all this scene of infantile satisfaction, Gustave Flaubert. ("Variation d'un paysage" [originally published 1982], *Travail de Flaubert*, ed. Gérard Genette and Tzvetan Todorov [Paris, 1983], 183)

20   Jean-Marie Privat, *Bovary charivari: essai d'ethno-critique* (Paris, 1994).

21   Jean Ricardou, *Nouveaux problèmes du roman* (Paris, 1978), 80. Emphasis in original.

22   Edi Zollinger, *Arachnes Rache. Flaubert inszeniert einen Wettkampf im narrativen Weben: "Madame Bovary" und "Notre-Dame de Paris" und der Arachne-Mythos* (Munich, 2007).

23   A. M. Lowe, "Emma Bovary, a modern Arachne," *French Studies* 26, no. 1 (January 1972): 30–41. Also pertinent to Zollinger's claims is a contribution to *La Production du sens chez Flaubert*, Jacques Seebacher's "Chiffres, dates, écritures, inscriptions," 286–96. I am deliberately foregoing specific page references to the different aspects of Zollinger's argument summarized in the text.

24   Luzius Keller, "Compte rendu de: Edi Zollinger, *Arachnes Rache, etc.*," *Flaubert: Revue critique et génétique* (25 October 2009), http://flaubert.revues.org/821.

25   Jean Starobinski, "L'Echelle des températures. Lecture du corps dans *Madame Bovary*" (originally published 1980), in Genette and Todorov, *Travail de Flaubert*, 45–78. Further page references will be in parentheses in the text.

26   Claude Duchet, "Roman et objets: l'exemple de *Madame Bovary*" (originally published 1969), in Genette and Todorov, *Travail de Flaubert*, 11–43. Further page references will be in parentheses in the text.

27   Jacques Neefs, "'Du réel écrit . . .'," *MLN* 122, no. 4 (September 2007): 697–712. Further page references will be in parentheses in the text.

28   Marcel Proust, "On Flaubert's Style," in *Against Sainte-Beuve and Other Essays*, trans. John Sturrock (London, 1988), 262. Further page references will be in parentheses in the text. For the original French see Philippot, 734.

29   Vladimir Nabokov, *Speak, Memory: An Autobiography Revisited* (London, 1967; New York and London, 1999), 134.

30   In *Madame Bovary*, at any rate. This is to disagree somewhat with Barthes's emphasis on the sentence, "la phrase," as at once "a unit of style, a unit of work, and a unit of life," which "attracts the essential quality of his confidences apropos his work as a writer" ("Flaubert et la phrase," in *Le Degré zéro de l'écriture: suivi de Nouveaux essais critiques* [Paris, 1953 and 1972], 137).

31   Steven Knapp, *Literary Interest: The Limits of Anti-Formalism* (Cambridge, Mass., 1993).

32   Two other personal factors may be worth mentioning. First, in writing about (so-called) English-language literary impressionists such as Stephen Crane and Joseph

Conrad, I have been led to pay close attention to the phonemic level of the texts under consideration. This is especially true of the chapter entitled "Stephen Crane's Upturned Faces" in *Realism, Writing, Disfiguration: On Thomas Eakins and Stephen Crane* (Chicago and London, 1987). The second factor concerns my activity as a poet, in particular as a writer of prose poems, in which effects of alliteration and consonance (and, no doubt, assonance) play a crucial role. See Michael Fried, *The Next Bend in the Road* (Chicago and London, 2004).

33   Readers familiar with the critical literature on Flaubert will recognize these sentences as ones singled out for analysis by Jonathan Culler in his landmark study *Flaubert: The Uses of Uncertainty*, rev. edn. (Ithaca and London, 1985), 75–7. Culler's aim is to demonstrate the oddness of those sentences with respect to several novelistic norms (which he does, persuasively), but the sheer density of alliterative patterning with respect to no fewer than six consonants (*t, b, f, p, m,* and *n*) either is not recognized or is not thought worthy of remark. Another, quite astonishing sentence of this type is found a page or so earlier: "La prairie s'allonge sous un bourrelet de collines basses pour se rattacher par-derrière aux pâturages du pays de Bray, tandis que, du côté de l'est, la plaine, montant doucement, va s'élargissant et étale à perte de vue ses blondes pièces de blé" (145). ["The pastures extend along the base of a chain of low hills and merge at the far end with the meadows of Bray; while eastward the plain rises gently and grows steadily wider, flaunting its golden grainfields as far as eye can see." (80)]

34   A sentence singled out for praise by Pierre Michon, " 'Le coup de génie de Flaubert," in "Les vies de *Madame Bovary*," ed. Jacques Neefs, special issue, *Le Magazine littéraire* no. 458 (November 2006): 39.

35   According to Jacques Neefs, this paragraph has come to be regarded as a "model" of Flaubertian description (Flaubert, *Madame Bovary*, 394n1). Neefs goes on to refer to a short, early instance of what will come to be known as "genetic" criticism by Albert Albalat in which the latter compares six successive versions of the paragraph in Flaubert's drafts as an example of the writer's manner of proceeding by continual gropings, crossings out, insertions, and expansions (in Albert Albalat, *Le Travail du style enseigné par les corrections manuscrites des grands écrivains* [Paris, 1909], 72–80). Interestingly, even the tentative first version contains multiple repetitions; by the third, something of the density of the final version is already in place. Neefs also refers to a short text by Gérard Genette in which he simply reproduces as a single continuous passage the six drafts of the paragraph without regard to crossings out or other notations ("Trois traitements de textes," in *Figures IV* [Paris, 1999], 351–4). The result is, as Neefs says, "strangely repetitive" but there is also a sense in which the manifest repetitions of words, phrases, and sentences serve to underscore, even to respond to, an even denser repetitive structure on the phonemic level.

36   And here is Lydia Davis's rendering of that sentence, in which (understandably) only one *v*-word survives: "Emma sat up like a corpse galvanized, her hair loose, her eyes

fixed and wide open" (Gustave Flaubert, *Madame Bovary: Provincial Ways*, trans. Lydia Davis [New York and London, 2010], 290).

37   The château of Vaubyessard belongs to the marquis d'Andervilliers (112), and while there Emma reads on the golden frames of two portraits of ancestors "Jean-Antoine d'Andervilliers d'Yverbonville, comte de la Vaubyessard et baron de la Fresnaye" and "Jean-Antoine-Henri-Guy d'Andervilliers de la Vaubyessard" (114), giving us several more *v*'s. We also learn from the text on the second frame that the subject of the portrait, an admiral of France, was wounded in the combat of Hougue-Saint-Vaast on 29 May 1692 and that he went on to die at Vaubyessard on 23 January ("janvier") 1693 (114–15). Something similar occurs early in part iii of the novel, when an officious Swiss guide insists on showing Emma and Léon certain features of the Cathedral of Rouen, where they had arranged to meet. Among those features are a simple paving stone covering the remains of "Pierre de Brézé, seigneur de la Varenne et de Brissac," and a statue of a knight in armor on a rearing horse marking the resting place of Pierre de Brézé's "petit-fils Louis de Brézé, seigneur de Breval et de Montchauvet, comte de Maulevrier, baron de Mauny, chambellan du roi, chevalier de l'Ordre et pareillement gouverneur de Normandie . . ." (368). ["This plain stone marks the resting place of Pierre de Brézé, lord of La Varenne and Brissac. . . . And on the right the nobleman in full armor on a rearing horse is his grandson Louis de Brézé, lord of Braval and Monchauvet, comte de Maulevrier, baron de Mauny, royal chamberlain, knight of the order and likewise governor of Normandy . . ." (275).] Slightly further on the guide remarks of another sculpture, "cette femme à genoux qui pleure est son épouse Diane de Poitiers, comtesse de Brézé, duchesse de Valentinois, née en 1499, morte en 1566; et, à gauche, celle qui porte un enfant, le sainte Vierge" (368) ["that weeping woman is his wife, Diane de Poitiers, comtesse de Brézé, duchesse de Valentinois, born 1499, died 1566; and on the left, holding a child, the Holy Virgin" (276)]. Throughout the paragraph in the text I have deliberately omitted page references in the interests of simplicity.

38   During the years of the composition of *Madame Bovary*, Flaubert took part, along with Louis Colet, in providing a secret "letter drop" for communications to and from Hugo in exile on Guernsey. See e.g., Gustave Flaubert to Victor Hugo, 2 June 1853, *Corr.*, 2:342–3.

39   See in this connection the Wikipedia article "Letter Frequency," http:// en.wikipedia.org/wiki/Letter_frequency, including the Frequency Distribution Graph for various languages including French. In fact there are eleven letters that occur less frequently than *v* in standard French prose, but the actual percentage (1.628%) is very low.

40   For the original French see *Corr.*, 2:691. Emphasis in original.

41   Albert Thibaudet, "Sur le style de Flaubert," in Philippot, 725.

42   For the original French see Philippot, 564. The previous paragraph reads:

It was not the novel such as the greatest had written, the novel in which one always feels something of the imagination and the author, the novel that could be classed among the tragic kind, the sentimental kind, the passionate or familial kind, the novel that showed the intentions, opinions, and manner of thought of the writer; [instead,] it was life itself that appeared. One would say that the personages arose under one's eyes in turning the pages, that the landscapes unrolled themselves with their sadnesses and their gaieties, their odors, their charm, that the objects too presented themselves to the reader as they were evoked by an invisible power, hidden who knows where. (Maupassant, "Gustave Flaubert: A Study," viii; translation modified.)

43   Ricardou, *Nouveaux problèmes du roman*, 80. Further page references will be in parentheses in the text.

44   Cf. in this connection Tony Tanner's discussion of still another series of words in play in the novel, one keyed to the morpheme (also the word) "cou," in English "neck" – "coudre," "coussinets," "couvrir," "coutume," "courbée," "coûter," "coups," "couds," "courir," "courbature," "cour," "coeur," etc. ("The 'Morselization' of Emma Bovary" [originally published 1979], in *Gustave Flaubert's "Madame Bovary,"* ed. Harold Bloom [New York, New Haven, and Philadelphia, 1988], 49–60). Tanner writes:

> I am not trying to suggest any shared etymology, some secret hidden original meaning which we can track down to the source, hoping to experience in its presence an etymic epiphany. I am no more hoping to intimate that all these words can be traced back somehow to the meaning "neck" than one would try to see the different parts of the body as having some common source in the physical neck. My point is literally of the most superficial kind – for I only want to draw attention to a surface phenomenon, namely that the same three letters appear in this cluster of words, modified of course by the other letters they are associated with, just as when spoken the same, or a very similar, sound may be heard, modified of course by the other sounds immediately succeeding or preceding it. (Flaubert, I think, did something similar with *rou* and arguably with *tou*, but I will concentrate on *cou*.) (53–4)

Tanner goes on, following Ferdinand de Saussure in his *Course in General Linguistics* (New York, 1959), to characterize such a chain as an "associative series" in contrast to syntagmatic relationships in which words are "chained together" to make individual sentences. He further suggests that marriage itself may be viewed as a syntagmatic relationship of a sort, whereas associative series stand for adultery. "Inasmuch as we all think in associative relations and speak in syntagms," he writes, then we may all be said to participate in these marital/adulterous aspects of language, the condition of being both absent and present, inside and outside discourse at the same time. Again, we must recognize that Emma's is not a unique but an exemplary case. She is inserted into a syntagmatic relationship, but her whole being tends to think and feel in (increasingly confused) associative constellations. Both of these modes of establishing relations are inherent in the language, indeed in *la condition linguistique*. They need not necessarily come into conflict or engender it, but the potential for doing so is always there, and in the figure of Emma Bovary, Flaubert concentrates on just that latent potentiality. (60)

This is ingenious, but the link with marriage and adultery seems to me tenuous at best. Not to mention the fact that Emma cannot be said to "own" all the associative relationships cited by Tanner. But he is on to something, nevertheless – the repetitiveness of *Madame Bovary* on the phonemic level.

A second project of Saussure's is relevant here. More precisely, I am thinking of Jean Starobinski's remarks in the penultimate paragraph of his fascinating little book about Saussure's purported discovery of patterns of phonemes in neoclassical Latin poetry and even prose that the great linguist took to refer to deliberately constructed anagrams of the names of Gods, a discovery that threatened to founder, indeed that ultimately did founder, owing to the sheer multiplicity of such relationships it seemed possible to detect. Starobinski writes: "Was Saussure mistaken? Did he allow himself to be fascinated by a mirage? Do his anagrams resemble the faces one can read in ink-blots? Perhaps Saussure's only mistake was to have posed the alternatives so sharply between 'chance' and 'conscious deliberation.' Under the circumstances, why not dismiss both chance and deliberation? Why should one not see in the anagram an aspect of human speech [*parole*] as it unfolds itself, in a way which is neither haphazard nor fully conscious? Why should there not be a repetition, a generative palilalia, which would project and multiply in discourse the raw ingredients of a primary word which is neither stated nor entirely suppressed? Short of being a conscious *rule*, the anagram can still be thought of as a *regularity* (or law) in which the arbitrary quantity of the theme-word is confined to the necessity of a procedure" (*Words upon Words: The Anagrams of Ferdinand de Saussure*, trans. Olivia Emmet [1971; New Haven and London, 1979], 122–3. Emphasis in original.).

Another possibility is suggested by Steven Knapp's notion of "literary interest" as developed in his brilliant book with that title. Toward the end he writes:

On the view I have defended in earlier chapters and in other writings, the object of literary *interpretation* is necessarily the meaning intended by some agent or collectivity of agents. But the object of literary *interest* is not an intended meaning; in fact, it isn't literally a *meaning* at all. The object of literary interest is a special kind of representational structure, each of whose elements acquires, by virtue of its connection with other elements, a network of associations inseparable from the representation itself. . . . But there is no reason why a structure eliciting an interest in the mutual implications of its elements can't be produced by accident, or by historical mechanisms transcending anyone's intentions. In this sense, a theorist like de Man can be wrong about literary language and still be right about the logic of literary overdetermination. And the New Critics, though wrong to think that literary interpretation could dispense with intention, were right in noticing that literary *interest* could do so. It isn't necessary, for the sake of literary interest, to settle on an intentional or non-intentional explanation – or *any* explanation – of how the relevant structure was produced. (Knapp, *Literary Interest*, 104. Emphasis in original.)

At no point in his study, with its emphasis on issues of representation, does Knapp consider the sorts of phonemic relationships that have been the focus of my concern in these pages. But his arguments in their generality do not seem to me invalidated by this omission, and it remains an open question to what extent they may be taken to bear on our topic; my impulse is to say that the sidestepping of the issue of intention he outlines doesn't quite fit the case. (Of course, a lot depends on what "transcending anyone's intentions" exactly means.) Knapp's reference to "earlier writings" is above all to his and Walter Benn Michaels's essay "Against Theory," originally published in *Critical Inquiry* 8, no. 4 (Summer 1982): 723–42.

45 For the original French see Du Bos, *Approximations*, 162–3.

46 For the original French see Philippot, 734. The *Trottoir roulant* was a technological innovation first exhibited with great success at the 1900 Exposition Universelle in Paris; in this connection see Sara Danius, *The Prose of the World: Flaubert and the Art of Making Things Visible* (Uppsala, 2006), 71. Danius, however, understands Proust's metaphor, and indeed Flaubert's project in *Madame Bovary*, in too exclusively visual a light.

47 For the original French see Philippot, 739–40.

48 I have changed the last sentence in Steegmuller's translation to register the fact that Canivet doesn't exactly say that it is all a question of habit but rather that Homais will say that it is. See the discussion of this passage in the text.

49 A recent bilingual French–English edition is Félix Ravaisson, *Of Habit*, trans. and ed. Clare Carlisle and Mark Sinclair (London and New York, 2008). Also in that volume are an "Editors' Introduction" (with a short biographical account), an "Editors' Commentary" (following the treatise), and a short essay by Catherine Malabou, "Addiction and Grace: Preface to Félix Ravaisson's *Of Habit*." The last of these persuasively resists Jacques Derrida's deconstructive reading of Ravaisson's treatise in *On Touching – Jean-Luc Nancy*, trans. C. Irizarry (Stanford, 2005). All in all, a very useful book.

Page references will be in parentheses in the text. See also Mark Sinclair, "Ravaisson and the Force of Habit," *Journal of the History of Philosophy* 49, no. 1 (January 2011): 65–85. Further page references will be given in parentheses in the notes.

50   Henri Bergson, "The Life and Work of Ravaisson," in *The Creative Mind: An Introduction to Metaphysics*, trans. Mabelle L. Andison (1946, 1974; New York, 1992), 220–52. Further page references will be in parentheses in the text.

51   Dominique Janicaud, *Ravaisson et la métaphysique. Une généalogie du spiritualisme français* (Paris, 1997), 48; an important study, from which I have learned much. Further page references will be in parentheses in the text.

52   See e.g., Gustave Flaubert to Louise Colet, 2 May 1852, *Corr.*, 2:82–3, in which he urges her to alter certain features of a character in her play *Les Lettres d'amour* (subsequently lost) so as not imply a resemblance to Cousin, whom he calls "le philosophe." Colet's affair with Cousin began in 1839; he may or may not have been the father of her daughter, Henriette, whom he helped support during the years when Colet was involved with Flaubert. See Jean Bruneau's notes to the letter mentioned above, 1063–4. Apparently a large number of letters between Cousin and Colet have still to be tapped as a scholarly resource (ibid., 1064).

53   For the original French see 26 July (?) 1857, *Corr.*, 2:749. The remark comes in a passage in which Flaubert explains to Feydeau that although he has been making great efforts in his research, historical accuracy is not the most important consideration for him:

> In any case, that matters very little, it's a secondary matter. A book can be full of howlers and blunders and be no less beautiful for that. Such a doctrine, if widely accepted, would be deplorable, I know, especially in France, where we have the pedantry of ignorance. But I see in the contrary tendency (which is mine, alas!) a great danger. The study of habit leads us to forget the soul. I would give the half-ream of notes that I've written over the past five months and the 98 volumes that I've read to be able, for no more than three seconds, to be *really* moved ["emotionné"] by the passion of my heroes. (Emphasis in original.)

54   Such a formulation may seem to fly in the teeth of Walter Benn Michaels's altogether persuasive argument to the effect that marks and sounds as such, being merely literal, are not linguistic at all (in *The Shape of the Signifier: 1967 to the End of History* [Princeton and Oxford, 2004], 51–66, 105–18). But from a Ravaissonian perspective we are asked to imagine will and intelligence extending, in however diminished and attenuated a form, to the realm of marks and sounds as such, thereby transforming them, if not into actual letters, at any rate into proto-linguistic entities of one sort or another. It should be obvious that the overall trajectory of this essay (indeed this book as a whole) is in accord with Michaels's views about meaning and intention in *The Shape of the Signifier*, "Against Theory," and elsewhere.

55 It is worth noting that *Madame Bovary* presents unmistakable instances of habit under-
    stood in a strictly negative sense. In the sixth of the exemplary passages cited previ-
    ously, for example, we are told: "L'amour [Emma's early infatuation with Léon], peu
    à peu, s'éteignit par l'absence, le regret s'étouffa sous l'habitude. . . ." Earlier, when
    Charles and Emma are still living in Tostes, her gradual disenchantment with her
    husband is described in similar terms:

> Quand elle eut ainsi un peu battu le briquet sur son coeur sans en faire jaillir
> une étincelle, incapable, du reste, de comprendre ce qu'elle n'éprouvait pas,
> comme de croire à tout ce qui ne se manifestait point par des formes convenues,
> elle se persuada sans peine que la passion de Charles n'avait plus rien d'exorbitant.
> Ses expansions étaient devenues régulières; il l'embrassait à de certaines heures.
> C'était une habitude parmi les autres, et comme un dessert prévu d'avance, après
> la monotonie du dîner. (110)

> Having thus failed to produce the slightest spark of love in herself, and since
> she was incapable of understanding what she didn't experience, or of recognizing
> anything that wasn't expressed in conventional terms, she reached the conclusion
> that Charles's desire for her was nothing very extraordinary. His transports had
> become regularized; he embraced her only at certain times. This had now become
> a habit like any other – like a dessert that could be counted on to end a monoto-
> nous meal. (49)

(A few pages before it is said of Charles: "Comme il avait eu longtemps l'habitude
du bonnet du coton, son foulard ne lui tenait pas aux oreilles" (108) ["He had so long
been used to wearing cotton nightcaps that he couldn't get his foulard to stay on his
head" (47)], a state of affairs it is implied Emma did not appreciate.) Habit, as it is
understood by Ravaisson, and as in my reading of *Madame Bovary* it is manifested as
a unifying principle at work throughout the novel on the plane of phonemic repetition, would be distinct from, indeed the very opposite of, this negative version. And
indeed, as we have seen, Canivet's use of the term in his exchange with Homais keeps
a distance from the latter. My thanks to Leonardo Lisi for inspiring these remarks.
    In this connection, it may or may not be significant that just before the famous
passage on Charles's "casquette," the text reads:

> Nous avions l'habitude, en entrant en classe, de jeter nos casquettes par terre, afin
> d'avoir ensuite nos mains plus libres; il faillait, dès le seuil de la porte, les lancer
> sous le banc, de façon à frapper contre la muraille en faisant beaucoup de pous-
> sière; c'était là le *genre*. (56)

> We always flung our caps on the floor when entering the classroom, to free our
> hands; we hurled them under the seats from the doorway itself, in such a way that
> they struck the wall and raised a cloud of dust: that was "how it was done." (4)

What strikes me as possibly significant is that the notion of habit thus figures so early in the novel, along with, on the following page, that of a "bredouillement de syllabes" (57) ["jumble of syllables" (5)] – the non-word "*Charbovari.*"

56   Michael Fried, *Courbet's Realism* (Chicago and London, 1990). I discuss Ravaisson on pp. 182–4, 187, 247, 272, 282, 309n14, 327–8n41, and 333n7. Further page references will be in parentheses in the text, though here too I will forego such references to the remarks about specific paintings I am about to make. For the historical background to my reading of Courbet, see Michael Fried, *Absorption and Theatricality: Painting and Beholder in the Age of Diderot* (1980; Chicago and London, 1987).

57   Linda Nochlin, "Courbet's Real Allegory: Rereading 'The Painter's Studio'," in *Courbet Reconsidered*, ed. Sarah Faunce and Linda Nochlin (Brooklyn, N.Y., 1988), 17–41. Exhibition catalogue. See in the same catalogue my essay "Courbet's 'Femininity'," in particular the postscript (a response to Nochlin), 52–3.

58   According to a contemporary witness, Francis Wey, Courbet painted the *After Dinner* while seated before it. See Fried, *Courbet's Realism*, 313n20.

59   René Huyghe, "Courbet," in *Gustave Courbet (1819–1877)* (Philadelphia and Boston, 1959–1960), n.p. Exhibition catalogue. Huyghe goes wrong, however, when he attributes Courbet's preoccupation with images of sleep to a wish "to place all nature on an equal footing, and to quench the spark of the spirit whenever it showed itself in a human being, so that nothing should disturb the worship of matter."

60   For a brief discussion of certain analogous features of Courbet's and Flaubert's respective relations to the products of their art, see Fried, *Courbet's Realism*, 267–70.

61   F. W. J. Schelling, *System of Transcendental Idealism (1800)*, trans. Peter Heath (Charlottesville, Va., 1978), 225.

62   Thus toward the end of the *System of Transcendental Idealism* Schelling states:

> If aesthetic intuition is merely intellectual intuition become objective, it is self-evident that art is at once the only true and eternal organ and document of philosophy, which ever and again continues to speak to us of what philosophy cannot depict in external form, namely the unconscious element [i.e., necessity] in acting and producing, and its original identity. Art is paramount to the philosopher, precisely because it opens up to him, as it were, the holy of holies, where burns in eternal and original unity, as if in a single flame, that which in nature and history is rent asunder, and in life and action, no less than in thought, must forever fly apart. The view of nature, which the philosopher frames artificially, is for art the original and natural one. (231–2).

In "Ravaisson and the Force of Habit," Mark Sinclair writes: "Habit, it should be noted, takes over the role that Schelling had ascribed to art in 1800 as 'the organon and document of philosophy' (*Sämtliche Werke*, ed. K. F. A. Schelling, vol. 3, *System des transcendentalen Idealismus* [Stuttgart, 1856–1861], 627), but the continuum revealed by reflection on habit differs markedly from the identity of spirit and nature that Schelling attempts to think within his system of transcendental idealism" (80n55). Sinclair goes on to cite various authors on the topic of Ravaisson's relation to Schelling. Among the writings I have found helpful in making sense of Schelling's aesthetics are Douglas W. Stott, "Translator's Introduction," in *The Philosophy of Art*, by F. W. J. Schelling, trans. Douglas W. Stott (Minneapolis, Minn., 1989), xxvii–xlv; David Simpson's "Foreword" to the same volume, ix–xxiv; the chapter on Schelling in Andrew Bowie, *Aesthetics and Subjectivity from Kant to Nietzsche*, 2nd ed. (Manchester and New York, 2003), 102–39; the one entitled "1795–1809: The Romantic Appropriation of Kant (II): Schelling," in Terry Pinkard, *German Philosophy 1760–1860: The Legacy of Idealism* (Cambridge and New York, 2002), 172–98; and the invaluable pages on Schelling's importance for Ravaisson and for later nineteenth-century French philosophy, in particular for Gabriel Séailles, Proust's teacher at the Sorbonne in 1894–1895, in Anne Henry, *Marcel Proust: Théories pour une esthétique* (Paris, 1981), 81–97, 131–5, and passim. Henry also documents Ravaisson's importance for Séailles and other French philosophers of his generation, hence, in crucial regards, for Proust; see in particular her citation of the account of the resources of spontaneous memory in Ravaisson's *Rapport sur la philosophie française* (133). I will only add that questions of habit or "second nature" remain a perennial problem for philosophy, as can be seen in the debates surrounding John McDowell's seminal *Mind and World* (Cambridge, Mass., and London, 1994). I am grateful to Leonardo Lisi and Robert B. Pippin for their invaluable assistance in coming even minimally to grips with these issues. Also to Ruth Leys for helpful conversations about McDowell and his critics.

63   Charles Baudelaire, "*Madame Bovary* par Gustave Flaubert" (originally published 1857), *Curiosités esthétiques. L'Art romantique et autres oeuvres critiques*, ed. Henri Lemaitre (Paris, 1962), 647–9. Further page references will be in parentheses in the text.

64   See, however, Naomi Schor, *Breaking the Chain: Women, Theory, and French Realist Fiction* (New York, 1985), esp. chap. 1, "For a Restricted Thematics: Writing, Speech, and Difference in *Madame Bovary*," 3–28. Schor gets under way by quoting Baudelaire: "In sum, this woman is truly great, she is above all pitiable, and in spite of the systematic hardness of the author, who has done everything possible to be absent from his work and to play the role of a master of marionnettes, all *intellectual* women owe him a debt of gratitutude for having elevated the female to such a high power, so far from the pure animal and so close to the ideal man" (6; my translation replacing an inadequate version in de Man, 341–2). For the original French see Baudelaire, "*Madame Bovary*," 649. Emphasis in original.

65   In *Courbet's Realism* I compare the distaff in the *Sleeping Spinner* with Baudelaire's treatment of a comparably "bi-gendered" object in his prose poem "Le Thyrse," ded-

icated and indeed addressed to Franz Liszt (198, fn). The staff of the thyrsus, Baudelaire writes, "c'est votre volonté" ["is your will"], the flowers wound around it, "c'est
la promenade de votre fantaisie autour de votre volonté; c'est l'élément feminin exé-
cutant autour du mâle ses prestigieuses pirouettes" ["is the promenade of your
fantasy around your will; it's the feminine element executing around the male
element its prestigious pirouettes"]. Charles Baudelaire, "Le Thyrse," *Le Spleen de
Paris. Petits poèmes en prose*, ed. Jean-Luc Steinmetz (Paris, 2003), 165–7.

66   My translation replacing an inadequate one in de Man, *Gustave Flaubert*. For the original French see Du Bos, *Approximations*, 156–7.

67   Ibid., 159.

68   *Corr.*, 2:30. Emphasis in original.

69   De Man, *Gustave Flaubert*, 363. Translation modified. For the original French see Du
Bos, *Approximations*, 160.

70   My translation replacing an inadequate one in de Man, *Gustave Flaubert*. For the original French see Du Bos, *Approximations*, 160.

71   See Jacques Neefs, "Le Flaubert de Charles Du Bos," *Flaubert: Revue critique et génétique* 1 (19 January 2009), http://flaubert.revues.org/544. For an extended and
insightful phenomenological treatment of related themes, see Jean-Pierre Richard,
"La création de la forme chez Flaubert," in *Stendhal et Flaubert: Littérature et sensation*
(1954; Paris, 1970), 137–252.

72   In this connection, I would not quite wish to say that Courbet's paintings lack "air"
in a sense analogous to Flaubert's prose as characterized by Du Bos. But it is nevertheless to the point that Courbet is the last of the great dark-ground painters, which
is to say that nowhere in his canvases do we find the sort of "blanks" that will start
to emerge in the art of Manet and his modernist successors, most notably, perhaps,
Paul Cézanne. My thanks to Jean-Pierre Criqui for his observations on this score.

73   In Philippot, 725.

74   Ibid., 722. Thibaudet's article begins by citing a polemic between Louis de Robert
and Paul Souday over the question "Flaubert savait-il écrire?" (Robert thought not,
Souday disagreed). For Thibaudet, Flaubert's many drafts themselves went to indicate that he was not "naturally a great writer" and that "plain verbal mastery was
not a gift he had naturally received" (for the original French see Philippot, 720). But
Flaubert had his strengths:

> People have mocked the "gueuloir" [Thibaudet writes]. Yet it is from this [device]
> that Flaubert drew all the refinement of his vocation. "Badly written sentences,"
> he says, "do not survive that test; they constrict the chest, impede the beating of
> the heart, and thus place themselves outside the condition of life." Through this,
> Flaubert found his way back to the great current of the classical style that . . . is a
> spoken style, associated with rhythms and the space of the voice. This is where

the substantial solidity of this Flaubertean form comes from, a form that will not age as long as there is a French language and that will remain muscled and perfect as a drawing by Ingres. (725)

In any case, Thibaudet acknowledges, Flaubert's style has proven itself by its fecundity, that is, its influence on an entire school of writers (726).

See in this connection the invaluable collection of essays by Robert, Souday, Thibaudet, Proust, and others edited by Gilles Philippe, *Flaubert savait-il écrire? Une querelle grammaticale (1919–21)* (Grenoble, 2004), as well as *idem, Sujet, verbe, complément. Le moment grammatical de la littérature française 1890–1940* (Paris, 2002).

75   See, most recently, Pierre-Marc de Biasi, *Gustave Flaubert. Une manière spéciale de vivre* (Paris, 2009), 39. De Biasi bases the association on a change in the spelling of the author's family name, introduced by his father, from Flobert to Flaubert; for the somewhat strained argument, see pp. 37–9. (The Flobert / Flaubert / Binet association was first suggested by Pierre Duymayet, "L'énigmatique carabinier Binet," *Le Magazine littéraire*, no. 401 [September 2001]: 36–40).

Binet, of course, makes napkin rings, in effect perfect zeros, on his lathe, an obsession that invites comparison with Flaubert's famous letter to Colet of 16 January 1852 beginning: "What seems beautiful to me, what I should like to write, is a book about nothing, a book dependent on nothing external, which would be held together by the internal strength of its style, just as the earth, suspended in the void, depends on nothing external for its support; a book which would have almost no subject, or at least in which the subject would be almost invisible, if such a thing is possible. The finest works are those that contain the least matter; the closer expression comes to thought, the closer language comes to coinciding and merging with it, the finer the result" (Steegmuller, *Letters of Gustave Flaubert*, 1:154; for the original French see *Corr.*, 2:31). One implication of the present essay is that *Madame Bovary* is not such a work.

76   Jonathan Culler, "The Realism of *Madame Bovary*," *MLN* 122, no. 4 (September 2007): 695. Further page references will be in parentheses in the text.

77   I owe to Yi-Ping Ong the suggestion that there may be a connection between the frequent occurrence in *Madame Bovary* of lists of various sorts and the sorts of micro-textual phenomena that I have been investigating, as if the serial nature of lists as well as, so to speak, the internal "replaceability" of the individual items they comprise amount to a kind of thematization of analogous aspects of those phenomena.

78   For the original French see Phillipot, 740.

79   Marcel Proust, "*L'Affaire Lemoine* par Gustave Flaubert," in *Ecrits sur l'art*, ed. Jérôme Picon (Paris, 1999), 269. Further page references will be in parentheses in the text and notes. First published in *Le Figaro (Supplément littéraire)*, 14 March 1908. For an argument that "Flaubert is omnipresent in Proust's work but always perfectly concealed" (from the back cover) see Mireille Naturel, *Proust et Flaubert. Un secret d'écriture* (1999;

Amsterdam and New York, 2007). See in particular the sections on the pastiches and the essay on Flaubert, pp. 63–93 and 95–108.

80   Marcel Proust, *The Lemoine Affair*, trans. Charlotte Mandell (Brooklyn, N.Y., 2008), 17. Further page references will be in parentheses in the text and notes. I might add that the role of habit in our affective lives is a major theme in Proust's *A la Recherche du temps perdu*, as has often been noted. See in this connection Amy Ross Loeserman, "Proust and the Discourse on Habit," (Ph.D. diss., University of Maryland, 2004).

81   Since we are, once again, on the topic of air, it just might be worth noting that in a letter to Colet of 25 June 1853 Flaubert wrote: "I would like to produce books which would entail only the *writing* of sentences (if I may put it that way), just as in order to live it is enough to breath the air" (Steegmuller, *Letters of Gustave Flaubert*, 1:189; *Corr.*, 2:362. Emphasis in original.). And in a letter to Hugo of 15 July 1853: "Exile, at least, spares you the sight of them [the monsters of public life in France]. Ah! if you knew into what filth we are plunged! Private infamies proceed from political turpitude and one can't take a step without stepping on something unclean. The atmosphere is heavy with nauseous vapors. Air! Air! For that, I open the window and turn toward you. I hear passing the great wing-beats of your Muse and I aspire [to breathe], as one might the fragrance of the forests, the exhalations that rise from the depths of your style" (*Corr.*, 2:382–3). The same outcry occurs in a different context in a letter to Colet of 21 May 1853 (*Corr.*, 2:328–32).

82   In this connection it is striking that toward the end of Proust's essay on Flaubert he turns abruptly to an analysis of a line of poetry by Sainte-Beuve (his *bête noire*), in order to show how the close repetition of three *r*-sounds "is awful if you stress the *r*'s and ridiculous if you roll them" (271). He continues:

> In general, the deliberate repetition of a vowel or a consonant can have grand effects (Racine: *Iphigénie, Phèdre*). A labial repeated six times in one line by Hugo conveys the impression of aerial lightness the poet is seeking to produce:
>
> > Les soufflés de la nuit flottaient sur Galgala.
>
> > The breezes of the night floated over Galgala.
>
> But then Hugo was able to exploit even the repetition of *r* sounds, which is on the contrary far from harmonious in French. At all events, whatever may be the case with verse, we no longer know how to read prose . . . (271–2) [For the original French, see Philippot, 742–3.]

One cannot help (at least I cannot help) wondering why the topic of repetitions of certain sounds suddenly and without obvious preparation engages Proust in this context.

Apropos Proust's pastiche of Flaubert, there are interesting observations in Gérard Genette, "Silences de Flaubert," in *Figures I* (Paris, 1966), 241.

83   For Flaubert's letter to Colet, which explains that the dead woman was the wife of a doctor who loved her dearly, and which goes on to justify his determination *"de profiter de tout"* [*"to profit from everything"*], see *Corr.*, 2:345–50. Emphasis in original.

84   By far the most serious study of contemporary responses to the *Burial* is by T. J. Clark, *Image of the People: Gustave Courbet and the Second French Republic, 1848–1851* (Greenwich, Conn., and London, 1973), 77–154.

85   Duranty's journal *Le Réalisme* ran from November 1856 to May 1857; he had not yet published his first novel, but his aesthetic commitments were significantly different from Flaubert's. So for example he wrote in the 15 December 1856 issue of his journal:

> That Realism wants nothing from its artists but the study of their times;
>
> That in the study of their times, it asks them not to distort anything but to preserve each thing's exact proportion;
>
> That the best way not to err in this study is always to think of the idea of representing the *social* side of the human being, which is the most visible, the most understandable, and the most varied, and thus to think of the idea of reproducing the things that influence the life of the greatest number, that happen often in the life of instincts, desires, and passions;
>
> That in this way Realism attributes to the artist a practical and useful philosophical goal, not one of entertainment, and in consequence elevates him;
>
> That in asking of the artist the *useful truth*, Realism asks of him above all feeling, the intelligent observation that *sees* a lesson, an emotion, in a spectacle of whatever kind . . .
>
> That the public is the decisive judge of the value of the *feelings* studied in a work because the masses are just as accessible to pity, misfortune, anger, etc. . . . as is the writer who addresses them . . . (Cited by Marcel Crouzet, *Un Méconnu du Réalisme: Duranty (1833–80)* [Paris, 1964], 438–9. Emphasis in original.)

Flaubert's response to these propositions, if ever they came his way, is not hard to imagine.

86   Charles-Augustin Sainte-Beuve, "*Salammbô*, par M. Gustave Flaubert," in Philippot, 198.

87   In a recent article, Shiguéhiko Hasumi observes that the name "Emma Bovary" never once appears in Flaubert's novel, and that this matters because it is precisely by signing the name "madame Bovary" on various legal documents that Emma exposes herself and her husband to the financial catastrophe that leads her to take her own life ("Absence d'Emma Bovary: *Réalité textuelle* de la fiction," *MLN* 125, no. 4 [September 2010]: 803–24). This is a nice point, but there is thus a sense in which it is only by dying, only with her death, that Emma becomes Emma Bovary, which pre-

sumably is the name engraved on her tomb (along with the grossly inappropriate Latin tag suggested by Homais; see Flaubert, *Madame Bovary*, 496).

88   For a while there was a question as to where Courbet would be allowed by the government of Napoleon III to erect his pavilion, but in the end "he was given permission to put his show exactly where he wanted it, on the avenue Montaigne, opposite the Palais des Beaux-Arts, 'at the very door of this Exposition,' as Fould had predicted [Achille Fould was Ministre d'état and therefore responsible for the exhibition; the reference is to a letter by Fould to the Préfet de Police]" (Patricia Mainardi, *Art and Politics of the Second Empire: The Universal Expositions of 1855 and 1867* [New Haven and London, 1987], 61).

On Flaubert and painting see Adrianne Tooke, *Flaubert and the Pictorial Arts: From Image to Text* (Oxford and New York, 2000). Tooke's book contains much valuable information but the pages she devotes to Courbet (43–4) fail to consider the possibility that, despite Flaubert's hostility to Realist ideas, he might have been struck by Courbet's art and in particular by the *Burial* (which she doesn't mention). By no means incidentally, she notes that Flaubert "copied out phrases from Courbet's famous alternative Exhibition catalogue of 1855 in the file entitled *Esthétique*, and these phrases were obviously intended to be used against Courbet in *Bouvard et Pécuchet*" (44). Quite possibly that was how Flaubert intended to make use of them, but the fact that he had transcribed them suggests that he might well have visited Courbet's one-man exhibition during his stay in Paris in late June and early July, 1855.

89   I owe to Angelo Careri the thought that *"cela pose un homme"* is italicized by Flaubert because it is one of those banal commonplaces he and his closest friends at once relished and mocked.

WILLING *SALAMMBÔ*

1   Late November 1857, *Corr.*, 2:783.

2   11 July 1858, ibid., 821. Emphasis in original.

3   For Froehner's article see *Corr.*, 3:1236–53; for Flaubert's reply see ibid., 293–301.

4   *Corr.*, 2:782–3. Emphasis in original.

5   Ibid., 794.

6   Ibid., 837. Emphasis in original.

7   Ibid., 845. Emphasis in original.

8   *Corr.*, 3:11. Emphasis in original.

9   Ibid., 17.

10   Ibid., 59.

11   Ibid., 122. In French the last clause reads: "et comme fond cela devient coquet."

12   Ibid., 165–6.

13   Ibid., 176.

14   Ibid., 195.

15   Gustave Flaubert, *Salammbô*, ed. Jacques Neefs (Paris, 2011), 430. Further page references will be in parentheses in the text and notes.

16   Gustave Flaubert, *Salammbô*, trans. A. J. Krailsheimer (London and New York, 1977), 282. Further page references will be in parentheses in the text.

17   See notably Jean Rousset, "Positions, distances, perspectives dans *Salammbô*," in *Travail de Flaubert*, ed. Gérard Genette and Tzvetan Todorov (Paris, 1983), 88–90; Rousset characterizes Flaubert's "c"était" ["it was"] as the instrument of an affirmation of the real, or indeed as of an "objective rectification" of a subjective perception.

18   See Marcel Proust, "A propos du 'style' de Flaubert," in Philippot, 735; actually, Proust's focus at this point in his essay is on *L'Education sentimentale*. Victor Brombert notes the reliance throughout *Salammbô* on the imperfect tense where the *passé simple* would seem natural (*The Novels of Flaubert: A Study of Themes and Techniques* [Princeton, 1966], 112).

19   See the ARTFL-FRANTEXT database for the occurrence of the word "cothurne" in French literary texts between 1800 and 1900. "The ARTFL Project," http://artfl-project.uchicago.edu/content/artfl-frantext. My thanks to Sue Waterman of the Milton S. Eisenhower Library at Johns Hopkins University for finding this source for me.

20   For Sainte-Beuve's articles see Philippot, 197–231. The passage quoted is from pp. 212–13. Further page references will be given in parentheses in the text.

21   Albert Thibaudet, *Flaubert* (1935; Paris, 1982), 131. See also ibid., 145–6.

22   On the self-enclosure or apartness of the world of the novel, see the important article by Rousset, "Positions, distances, perspectives dans *Salammbô*," in which the critic draws attention to the artful control of points of view throughout the narrative, emphasizing in particular the symmetry between Mâtho's gaze up toward the descending Salammbô in the opening chapter and, in the last pages of the final chapter, Mâtho's agonizing descent from the summit of the acropolis, culminating in an exchange of gazes with Salammbô closely followed by the deaths of both (80–82).

23   See e.g., Gustave Flaubert to Jules Duplan, 24 June 1862, *Corr.*, 3: 226.

24   Ibid., 278.

25   Cf. Michel Butor: "What are twelve kinds of emeralds? It's up to us to invent them" ("Demeures et dieux à Carthage." *Corps écrit* 9 [1984]: 135) – but of course we can't. Butor also remarks on Flaubert's insistence on referring to geographical locations by their ancient rather than their modern names, and unclassical ones at that – for Gibraltar not the columns of Hercules, which would have been understood, but what

Flaubert took to be the punic equivalent, Melkart (130–31). Moreover, in at least one instance in which Flaubert does explain the meaning of foreign terms – the names of the siege engines brought to bear against Carthage (332, 334) – the explanations come *after* the terms themselves are wielded for the first time (327).

26   What Flaubert says is that for the Numidian name of Naravasse "I wrote Narr'Havas, from *Nar-el-hawa*, fire of the breath" (21 January 1863, *Corr.*, 3:294).

27   In the course of the discussion following Jacques Neefs's "Le Parcours du zaïmph" in *La Production du sens chez Flaubert*, Colloque de Cerisy, ed. Claudine Gothot-Mersch (Paris, 1975), Claude Duchet calls attention to the graphic and phonic strangeness of the word "zaïmph," to which Neefs replies, "As far as the overdetermination of the zaïmph on the level of the signifier [Duchet's suggestion] is concerned, I completely agree with you. If the signifier captures our attention, it is above all, I think, because it includes letters that are rare in the French alphabet, the Z at the beginning, the final PH, and ï in the middle.

> Philippe Hamon: Z and PH are phonemes that have very negative connotations in everyday speech; if you articulate badly it's frowned on [si vous zozottez ou si vous phophottez, c'est très mal vu].

> Jacques Neefs: An unpronounceable word, then. I have searched vainly for its origin. In the brouillons reproduced in the Club de l'honnête homme edition, Flaubert constantly speaks of the peplos, the veil of the goddess, and all of a sudden the zaïmph appears, without explanation. (248–9)

28   Guy de Maupassant was later to write of *Salammbô*: "Is it a novel? Isn't it rather a sort of opera in prose? The tableaux develop with a prodigious magnificence, a brilliance, a color, and a rhythm that surprise one" ("Gustave Flaubert [Extraits], preface to *Lettres de Gustave Flaubert à George Sand* [originally published 1884], in Philippot, 567).

29   For my use of the concept of "mimesis" in this context to stand for something like hypnotic suggestiveness, see Mikkel Borch-Jacobsen, *The Freudian Subject*, trans. Catherine Porter (Stanford, 1988); *idem*, *The Emotional Tie: Psychoanalysis, Mimesis, and Affect*, trans. Douglas Brick et al. (Stanford, 1993); and Ruth Leys, *Trauma: A Genealogy* (Chicago and London, 2000).

30   The word "orgueil," a bit surprising in this context, recurs at a later moment, when Salammbô in effect presents herself to Mâtho in his tent. A page or so before their sexual encounter we read: "Mâtho se leva d'un bond; un orgueil colossal lui gonflait le coeur; il se trouvait haussé à la taille d'un Dieu" (293). ["Mâtho sprang up; enormous pride filled his heart; he felt raised to the stature of a God" (184).] The repetition of "orgueil" as an (almost Racinian) euphemism for sexual excitement or indeed for an erection is typical of the extraordinarily artful construction of the novel as a whole.

31   Charles Baudelaire, "Théophile Gautier," in *Curiosités esthétiques. L'Art romantique et autres oeuvres critiques*, ed. Henri Lemaitre (Paris, 1962), 679. Originally published in *L'Artiste*, 13 March 1859.

32   See the *Journal* entry for 6 May 1861, cited by Philippot, 194. Further page references will be given in parentheses in the text.

33   Théophile Gautier, "*Salammbô* [Extraits]," from Philippot, 259. Further page references will be in parentheses in the text.

34   There are interesting remarks on description in *Salammbô* as evocative of absolute otherness or alterity in Jacques Neefs, "*Salammbô*, textes critiques," *Littérature* 15 (1974): 53–64; also in Lawrence R. Schehr, "*Salammbô* as the Novel of Alterity," *Nineteenth-Century French Studies* 17 (1989): 26–41; and *idem*, *Figures of Alterity: French Realism and Its Others* (Stanford, 2003), 96–143, if one can ignore the latter texts' more "theoretical" moments.

35   The charge of immobility goes back to Alcide Dusolier in his strongly critical review, "*Salammbô*, par M. Gustave Flaubert" (in Philippot, 265–72), but it has been taken up by modern commentators such as Victor Brombert and J. R. Dugan, among others. See Brombert, "*Salammbô*: The Epic of Immobility," chap. 3 in *The Novels of Flaubert*, 92–124; and J. R. Dugan, "Flaubert's *Salammbô*, A Study in Immobility," *Zeitschrift für französische Sprache und Literatur* 79, no. 3 (1969): 193–206.

36   In the review just cited, Dusolier has nothing but harsh words for Flaubert's "fury of description" (268), including the interesting remark, "Monsieur Flaubert sees everything only through a stereoscope" (268), a crucial feature of stereoscopic photographs being that the separate planes are all in sharp focus.

37   On Baudelaire and crowds see e.g., Yves Bonnefoy, *Le poète et "le flot mouvant des multitudes." Paris pour Nerval et pour Baudelaire* (Paris, 2003), 73–147. In a highly favorable review of *Salammbô*, the critic Paul de Saint-Victor cites Poe's story and says of Flaubert that he "would merit that name" (the Man of the Crowds) on the strength of his depiction of crowds and multitudes ("*Salammbô*, par M. Gustave Flaubert," in Philippot, 245). Throughout chapter thirteen of *Salammbô*, the long and brutal account of the worst of the siege of Carthage, the words "foule" and "multitude" occur frequently, as Flaubert could not have failed to be aware.

38   Apropos of these sentences Jacques Neefs writes: "Writing must be capable of making the paper howl: the hand that saturates the page, and a mouth that howls, make the silent cry that is imprinted on the pages. One can imagine that to 'gueuler' sentences while writing has the same function for Flaubert . . ." ("Colères de Flaubert," in *Colères d'écrivains*, ed. Martine Boyer-Weinmann and Jean-Pierre Martin [Nantes, 2009], 162–3).

39   The epithet is Sainte-Beuve's in his second article (217), to which Flaubert replies that he felt slightly wounded by it, apparently because he feared being publicly stigma-

tized as a disciple of the Marquis de Sade (*Corr.*, 3:81–2). See, however, the Goncourts' *Journal* entry for an unspecified date in November 1858 where we read: "Flaubert, a mind haunted by Monsieur de Sade, to whom he always returns as if to an enticing mystery" (Goncourt and Goncourt, *Journal*, 1: 867); the same entry reports: "For his novel, he has chosen Carthage as the most rotten of places and civilizations. In six months, he has completed only two chapters, which are a brothel of little boys and a mercenaries' meal . . ." (868). (Later entries, too, record Flaubert's fascination with Sade.) See also Claire-Lise Tondeur, "Flaubert et Sade, ou la fascination de l'excès," *Nineteenth-Century French Studies* 10 (Fall–Winter 1981–2): 75–84.

40   See Flaubert's letter to Feydeau of 16 August 1857, in which he says of the latter's novel *L'été* that "it seems to me that its partiality, its intention, are too visible, the artist can be sensed behind the canvas" (*Corr.*, 2:753). And a letter of 29 November 1859, also to Feydeau, in which he writes: "When people read *Salammbô*, they won't, I hope, think of the author. Few people will guess how sad one needed to be to undertake the resurrection of Carthage. It [the novel] is a Thebiad to which I've been pushed by disgust with modern life" (*Corr.*, 3:59).

41   After the retaking of Tunis from mercenaries, the extensive destruction includes the corpses of numerous elephants killed in the struggle. The text continues: "Le peuple, qui les avait vus de loin périr, en fut désolé; des hommes se lamentaient dans les rues en les appelant par leurs noms, comme des amis défunts: – 'Ah! l'Invincible! la Victoire! le Foudroyant! l'Hirondelle!'" (407) ["The people, who had seen them perish in the distance, were deeply grieved; men went about the streets lamenting and calling them by their names, like dead friends: 'Oh! Invincible! Victory! Foudroyant! Swallow!'" (266–7)]. That the last name seems out of keeping with the three preceding ones makes its reference back to *Madame Bovary* all the more striking.

42   There are also moments in the Flaubert's letters that resonate with ones in the novel, as when he writes to Feydeau on 28 August 1858: "Sometimes I feel so sad, I could croak. There you have it! / Which does not keep me from roaring from morning to evening, so as to burst my chest" (*Corr.*, 2:830). The last sentence in French: "Ce qui ne m'empêche pas de hurler du matin au soir, à me casser la poitrine."

43   See e.g., Jeanne Bem, "Modernité de 'Salammbô'," *Littérature* 40 (1980): 18–31; Françoise Gaillard, "La Révolte contre la Révolution. *Salammbô*: Un autre point de vue sur l'histoire," in *Gustave Flaubert*, ed. A. de Toro (Tübingen, 1987), 43–54; Eugenio Donato, "*Flaubert* and the Question of History" (originally published 1976), in *Critical Essays on Flaubert*, ed. L. M. Porter (Boston, 1986), 87–103; Jacques Neefs, "Préface," in Flaubert, *Salammbô*, 33; and the critical discussion of this issue in Joachim Küpper, "Considérations sur *Salammbô*," *MLN* 125, no. 4 (September 2010): 764n14, 776n69. Küpper's article offers an invaluable tour d'horizon of the secondary literature on *Salammbô*.

44   An influential article that broke new ground in this regard is Neefs, "Le Parcours du Zaïmph." See also Küpper's persuasive analysis of the progressive demystification of the myths in the course of the novel in "Considérations sur *Salammbô*," 752–7.

45   Charles-Augustin Sainte-Beuve, "*Madame Bovary*, par M. Gustave Flaubert," in Philippot, 139.

46   Neefs, "Préface," 32–3.

47   As we saw in "Style and Habit in *Madame Bovary*," Neefs in a recent essay also characterized the prose of *Madame Bovary* as calling for "a kind of assent to the fiction, assent to its sensory [the French is "sensible"], rhythmic, profound details," which is to say to a "mental and sensory participation of an altogether new type" ("'Du réel écrit . . .'," *MLN* 122, no. 4 [September 2007]: 707). This suggests that in both novels something like a specific act of readerly "assent" is called for, the crucial difference being that in the case of *Salammbô* what must be "assented" to is more arduous, confrontational, against the grain – in short, "willfully harassing."

48   On the topic of description Küpper writes pertinently: "The descriptions – and more precisely, their unsettling character and the redundancy effect that results from it – explain the distance between *Salammbô* and the novelistic projects of the twentieth century that are grouped under the heading of *realismo mágico* and *real marvilloso*, with which our text shares a number of characteristics. To further develop this argument, one would need to show how in these cases, inventories are devised only to the extent to which they can serve the reader as 'exotic potions' (Valéry on M. A. Asturias). In Flaubert, in contrast, the invasion of the reader's consciousness by 'foreign' elements is – at least so I claim – willed as such in order to do away with the desire to escape into the distance" ("Considérations sur *Salammbô*," 774n60).

49   For example, Dusolier, who finds even *Madame Bovary* primarily a work of patience and "volonté" rather than genius ("*Salammbô*, par M. Gustave Flaubert," in Philippot, 265). "One perpetually feels the effort and the tension," he complains, "Monsieur Flaubert lacks that supreme ease that is the sign of the truly great" (267), thereby anticipating some of the criticisms that were later raised about Flaubert's prose by Thibaudet and others (see above, "Style and Habit in *Madame Bovary*," pp. 90–91 and n. 74). As he also writes of both novels, "Effort, always effort: not a line that is not an arduous construction; each noun, each epithet is like a heavy stone carried onto the scaffolding by the bent-over laborer" (272). Flaubert might well agree: see the great and scornful "pyramid" image in the first of the two epigraphs to the present essay.

50   In 1880, however, after Flaubert's death, Théodore de Banville wrote admiringly: "With a new masterpiece, this marvelous *Salammbô*, which is the true epic story of modern times, [Flaubert] proved that experimental and scientific analysis can be applied even to things that no longer exist and that have not, so to speak, left a single

trace. Carthage, Hamilcar's Carthage, with its gods, human sacrifices, horrible battles, an entire civilization gone, an entire ancient world submerged in the three-fold night of time, forgetting, and ruins, was resuscitated by the evocation of a will that would not be discouraged by anything . . ." ("Gustave Flaubert [Extraits]," in Philippot, 448).

51 Michael Fried, *Manet's Modernism, or, The Face of Painting in the 1860s* (Chicago and London, 1996), 186–97. Further page references will be in parentheses in the text.

52 23–24 December 1862, *Corr.*, 3:282. Emphasis in original.

53 Veronica Forrest-Thomson, "The Ritual of Reading 'Salammbô'," *The Modern Language Review* 67, no. 4 (October 1972): 792. See also Peter Starr, "*Salammbô*: The Politics of an Ending," *French Forum* 10 (January 1985): 40–56. Further page references to Starr's article will be in parentheses in the text.

54 Gustave Flaubert, 12 July 1862. *Corr.*, 3: 229–30.

55 Charles Baudelaire, *Correspondance*, ed. Claude Pichois with Jean Ziegler (Paris, 1973), 2:473. Emphasis added. Cited by Jean-Luc Steinmetz, "Préface," in *Le Spleen de Paris. Petits poèmes en prose*, by Charles Baudelaire, ed. Jean-Luc Steinmetz (Paris, 2003), 17.

56 An early crux in this regard is the marvelously original discussion of William Haus-soullier's *Fontaine de Jouvence* in his Salon of 1845 (in Baudelaire, *Curiosités esthétiques. L'Art romantique*, 15–19). See also Michael Fried, "Painting Memories: On the Containment of the Past in Baudelaire and Manet," *Critical Inquiry* 10, no. 3 (March 1984): 510–42.

57 Charles Baudelaire, "A Arsène Houssaye," in *Le Spleen de Paris*, 61. Emphasis in original. At the same time, the previous aesthetic of masking or otherwise transcending "volonté" is clearly expressed in one of the most arresting prose poems, "Une mort héroique," in which the merely good actor is described as one who, "sous le personnage, se laisse encore deviner le comédien, c'est-à-dire l'art, l'effort, la volonté" ["beneath the character, allows one to detect the actor, that is to say art, effort, will"] (141). Whereas the perfect actor, in this case the clown Fancioulle giving his last performance under the threat of death, is compared hyperbolically to "les meilleures statues de l'antiquité" ["the best statues of antiquity"] miraculously come alive, not that we should take the invocation of antiquity wholly seriously.

58 Baudelaire to Louis Marcelin, editor of *La Vie Parisienne*, in a letter of 10 November 1864: "I hope I can make amends to you with a bundle of *Poèmes en prose*. I have a good thirty of them on my desk; but they are horrors and monstrosities that will cause abortions in your pregnant readers" (*Correspondance*, 2:465; cited by Steinmetz, "Préface," 17). Again, we should be on guard against taking Baudelaire at his word – irony was a preferred literary mode, nowhere more so than in the prose poems themselves. But of course irony such as his cuts against the reader fully as much as against himself. "Nothing in *Le Spleen de Paris* offers the mind ["esprit"] the virtue of

some enduring compensation," Steinmetz writes. "With a malignity that may without exaggeration be considered satanic, Baudelaire sets out to destroy any euphoric and gratifying image. It is clear that he composed while essentially moved by a preoccupation to disillusion our gaze and undermine our hope" ("Préface," 35).

One of the prose poems, "Les Tentations," might just contain a glancing reference to *Salammbô*. The first of three "Satanic" figures (a male) is partly described as follows: "A ses chevilles délicates traînaient quelques anneaux d'une chaîne d'or rompue, et quand la gêne qui en résultait le forçait à baisser les yeux vers la terre, il contemplait vaniteusement les ongles de ses pieds, brillants et polis comme des pierres bien travaillées" (*Le Spleen de Paris*, 119–20). ["His delicate ankles trailed some rings of a broken golden chain, and when the annoyance that resulted from this forced him to lower his eyes toward the ground, I contemplated with vanity the toenails of his feet, brilliant and polished like heavily worked stones."] I am thinking mainly of the broken "chaînette", of course, but the gemlike toenails too might have stepped forth from Flaubert's novel.

59 What might a literary text be like that aimed to go beyond both *Salammbô* and *Le Spleen de Paris* in the direction of explicitly and with great gusto thematizing an aggressive or say openly "cruel" relation to the reader? One candidate: the comte de Lautréamont's [Isidore Ducasse's] *Chants de Maldoror*, the first canto of which was printed at the author's expense in 1868, just six years after the appearance of Flaubert's second novel.

60 "Finally, after some twenty years of fruitless research across the various disciplines, disgusted with everything and in particular with what they consider to be the contradictions and excessive pretentions of science, the two supernumeraries regain their joy of life only by going back to their initial occupation: copying. 'No reflection! let's copy! The page must be filled, "the monument" be completed. – equality of everything, of good and evil, the beautiful and the ugly, the insignificant and the characteristic. Nothing is true but phenomena. – End with the sight of the two fellows bent over their desk, copying'" (Scénario autographe pour la conclusion, non rédigée, MS gg 10, fol. 67). Pierre-Marc de Biasi, "Le Galaxie *Bouvard et Pécuchet*, introduction to Gustave Flaubert, *Bouvard et Pécuchet* (Paris, 1999), 10–11.

61 *Corr.*, 2: 699. Emphasis in original.

62 *Corr.*, 3: 26. Emphasis in original.

63 *Corr.*, 2: 716. Emphasis in original.

64 Ibid., 716. At an earlier moment, Flaubert responds vigorously to his correspondent's account of her religious doubts and hesitations. "Here is what I was thinking: you must try to be more Catholic or more philosophical. You have read too much to sincerely believe. Don't you object! you would very much like to believe. That's all there is to say. . . . Therefore, be frank with yourself. Make a supreme effort, an effort that

will save you. You must take either all of the *one* or all of the *other*. In the name of
Christ, don't remain sacrilegious out of fear of irreligion! In the name of philosophy,
don't degrade yourself in the name of that weakness we call habit. Throw everything over-
board, for the ship is sinking" (30 March 1857, *Corr.*, 2:699. Emphasis added.). Also:
"What can I do for you other than repeat to you the very advice you don't follow:
quit your habitual life . . ." (18 January 1862, *Corr.*, 3:198. Emphasis in original.).

65 Elias Canetti, *Crowds and Power*, trans. Carol Stewart (London, 1962), 305–6, 316–19.

66 See in this connection Walter Benn Michaels, "Action and Accident: Photography and
Writing," Chap. 7 in *The Gold Standard and the Logic of Naturalism: American Literature
at the Turn of the Century* (Berkeley, Los Angeles, London, 1987), 215–44; *idem*, "Photography and Fossils," in *Photography Theory* ed. James Elkins (New York and London,
2007), 431–50; *idem*, "Neoliberal Aesthetics: Fried, Rancière and the Form of the
Photograph," *nonsite.org* 1(25 January 2011), http://nonsite.org/issues/issue-1/
neoliberal-aesthetics-fried-ranciere-and-the-form-of-the-photograph; and Michael
Fried, "Barthes's *Punctum*," chap. 4 in *Why Photography Matters as Art as Never Before*
(New Haven and London, 2008), 95–114, 261–81 (on Thomas Demand's photo-
graphic "allegories of intention" and on Thomas Struth's early cityscapes) and 335–
47 (on Michaels, Barthes, and the question of antitheatricality). Increasingly, the
thematization of intention has emerged as central to significant works of contem-
porary art, such as Anri Sala's video *Mixed Behavior* (2004), Charles Ray's sculpture
Hinoki (2007), and Thomas Demand's stop-motion film *Pacific Sun* (2012). See
Michael Fried, "Sala with Schiller: World, Form, and Play in *Mixed Behavior*," in *Anri
Sala*, exh. cat. (London, 2011), 97–104, and *nonsite.org* 5; *idem*, *Four Honest Outlaws:
Sala, Ray, Marioni, and Gordon* (New Haven and London, 2011), 91–103 (on Ray's
Hinoki); and *idem*, "Thomas Demand's *Pacific Sun*," in *Thomas Demand: Animations*,
exh. cat. (Des Moines, 2012). In an important sense, Flaubert's project in *Salammbô*
has never been more *current*.

INDEX

PHOTOGRAPH CREDITS